HEREFORDSHIRE PUBS

JOHN EISEL AND RON SHOESMITH

The History Press

Front cover: A jolly party outside the Orange Tree,
Hereford, in the late nineteenth century.
(Derek Foxton Collection)

First published 2009

The History Press
The Mill, Brimscombe Port
Stroud, Gloucestershire, GL5 2QG
www.thehistorypress.co.uk

ISBN 978 0 7524 4466 6

Typesetting and origination by The History Press
Printed in Great Britain

CONTENTS

ACKNOWLEDGEMENTS

Over a period of years the pubs of Herefordshire have been covered in a series of five books, starting with those in the city of Hereford, and the authors have been much involved in this series. This title is a distillation of those five books, and we are most grateful to our fellow authors, Heather Hurley, Roger Barrett and Frank Bennett, who have allowed us to use without restriction material from their publications. Of course, in the nature of things, more information has come to light since publication, and the opportunity has been taken to include as much of this as practicable within the limited space available. We should also like to put on record our gratitude to the staff of Hereford Reference Library and Hereford Record Office, where much of the documentary research was performed, and also to those who kindly passed on information either verbally or in writing. This type of book is essentially an illustrated record, and these old photographs have been taken from a wide range of sources. We are most grateful for the permission to use them. The sources of the illustrations are given below with their page number and 't' or'b' indicating their position at the top or bottom of the page. Except for a few whose source cannot be determined, the remainder are from the authors' collections.

Hereford Reference Library: 10, 13t&b,16t, 24b, 26t, 27b, 31b, 37b, 48t, 57t, 58b, 78b, 84b, 115b, 120t&b
Hereford Record Office: 44, 78t, 94b, 104b, 126t
Hereford City Museum: 9, 14, 23t
Bromyard Local History Society: 53, 55l, 57b, 62t,73t
Ledbury and District Society Trust Ltd.: 68t
Woolhope Club Transactions; 75b, 93b
Ross Heritage Centre: 79t
Gloucester Record Office: 80tl
Hereford Times: 124b
Chase Hotel: 88t
Ross Gazette: 88m
St Peter's Bellringers, Bromyard: 60b
Tim Ward: 65, 71tl, 75t, 76b, 81t, 84t, 85b, 95b, 97, 99t, 100b, 108t, 109t, 116t, 124t
Heather Hurley: 77, 79b, 80tr&b, 82, 83, 85t, 86t&b, 88br, 89t&b, 90b, 91t&b, 92, 94t, 95t, 96t, 100t
Frank Bennett: 12, 41m, 58t, 104t, 111, 114b
Derek Foxton: Outer cover, 15t, 16b, 24t, 27t, 102t
John Hartwright: 54t&b
Ken Hoverd: 19b
Agnes Jones: 61t&b
David Garrett Village Archive: 125t&m
The late Mrs Gittins: 22b
Brian Burrell: 108b
Andy Johnson: 110t
Anne Sandford Estate: 122b

INTRODUCTION

In the following pages are found a selection of photographs and descriptions of pubs in Herefordshire. Within the limitations of the length of this book, it is impossible to include them all, so a selection has had to be made in order to give an overall picture. This selection is a personal one, made by us, and probably someone else would have made a different one, but there would be much in common between the two lists. Most of the illustrations are old, but there is a proportion of recent photographs, and to give a better overview we have included some pubs that were prominent in their day, but have now closed. This book tells something of the story of how pubs fitted into society in their day, and so must be counted to some extent as a book of social history. There are many fascinating stories associated with pubs, and some have been included to make the book of more general interest. Even without them, we are sure that the photographs themselves make the book worthy of place on the bookshelves of anyone interested in Herefordshire itself or even just in pubs generally!

In early times, alehouses were a place where men could get away from the realities of life, and discuss matters of mutual interest in a convivial atmosphere. Such places brewed their own ale, and this seems to have been part of the domestic duties, for the Domesday Book of 1086 recorded that any man's wife who brewed ale inside or outside the city of Hereford gave 10s. as a customary due. One of the provisions of Magna Carta in 1215 was that there should be standard measures of wine, ale and corn. The importance of bread and ale as necessities of life was recognized in the Assize of Bread and Wine in 1266, which ensured that the retail price of ale was fixed according to the price of grain from which it was made. Ale was brewed from malt made from grain, whilst beer is flavoured with hops. These were introduced in the early fifteenth century, and were described by the authorities in Shrewsbury at the time as that 'wicked and pernicious weed'. The hop not only gave the new drink a more bitter flavour but also its preservative properties enabled beer to be kept much longer than ale before 'going off'. Not that these advantages were appreciated immediately, and in the sixteenth century there was a Hereford city regulation that any brewer who put hops or ashes into their ale would be fined 20s,, a severe penalty at the time. In 1554 city regulations fixed the cost of a sester (four gallons) of 'good & able Ale & bere' at 20d but by 1557 this had gone up to 2s. By 1576 this had gone up further to 2s 6d, so inflation is nothing new!

The regular customers of early alehouses would in general have no need to travel; indeed in medieval times those who travelled would normally be of the upper classes and their retinues. If they wanted accommodation overnight they would stay at a convenient religious house, which had a duty to provide accommodation for travellers. In later medieval times there were more merchants travelling than previously, and so this gave rise to the wayside inns and hostelries in towns, which provided accommodation and food as well as liquid sustenance. With the dissolution of the religious houses in the 1530s the inn received a boost and no doubt many started to provide a higher standard of accommodation. Another word that also had a specific meaning was 'tavern', which in the sixteenth century and before indicated that wine was sold as well as ale and beer, but did not necessarily mean that accommodation was offered. Thus a tavern was of higher status, and in 1553 the number of taverns was limited by Act of Parliament. Hereford was limited to three. But the meaning of the word has changed as it is often now used in a deprecating sense, and a tavern calls up an image of low-life.

Curiously, there was a survival of the earlier specific usage in Hereford – in High Town until the middle of the nineteenth century there was what was generally referred to as the Sun Tavern Inn!

Attempts at licensing alehouses began at the end of the fifteenth century, and in the sixteenth century the Justices obtained the power not only to license premises but to suppress them as well. Also, since any pleasure is seen as a source income by the government, at the time of the Civil Wars in the middle of the seventeenth century, attempts were made to tax beer, ale and cider. Beer came in three strengths, strong, table, and small, each of which was taxed differently. Cider, of course, was a product of the county and much drunk not only by the working classes, but also as a vintage drink by the upper classes, the usual spelling being 'cyder'. From a surprisingly early date cider was sent long distances, even as far as London. First it was sent in barrels, but the boastful Andrew Yarranton, in his book *England's Improvement by Land and Sea*, the first edition of which was published in 1677, claimed credit for himself and his business partner for bottling 'sider' and sending large quantities to London via Gloucester and Lechlade. Whatever the truth of this, there is no doubt that in the eighteenth century large quantities of cider were sent down river from Hereford.

Cider had been taxed from time to time, but in 1763 an increased tax was introduced, to be levied on the makers. This caused an outcry and later that year the Common Council of Hereford resolved to petition Parliament to have the duty lifted. This finally happened early in 1766 and there was much rejoicing in the county. In Hereford there was a bonfire in celebration, with accompanying music from drums and fifes, and fireworks, all paid for by the public purse.

At the end of the seventeenth century cheap brandy and the introduction of gin had an impact on the larger centres of population, with a huge increase in consumption of spirits in the next century, the effects of which were graphically illustrated by William Hogarth. Various Gin Acts and stronger powers for the magistrates eventually reduced consumption from over 8 million gallons in 1743 to less than 2 million gallons a year in 1758. However, it is likely that, apart from increased regulation, this had little effect on Herefordshire.

What did have an effect was the gradual improvement in the roads in the eighteenth century, with various Turnpike Acts. Firstly, the trustees had to meet somewhere to discuss their business – and where better than the local inn, with liquid refreshment paid for by someone else? And then the tolls for the various gates had to be let by auction, and a place was needed to hold that auction. Each turnpike trust had its regular place of meeting; for example, for a period of nearly 200 years the Presteigne and Blue Mantle Hall Turnpike Trusts met regularly at the Mortimer's Cross Inn at Aymestrey. Then, of course, with the improved roads there was much more travel, with a need for accommodation and a place to change horses, or indeed to hire a post-chaise.

For the larger inns, there was usually a large assembly room where important functions could be held. The Assembly in Bromyard was held in the winter months in the large room at the Falcon, while the Great Room at the City Arms in Hereford – an establishment so well known that from the early part of the nineteenth century it was just known as the 'Hotel' – held a reception for Nelson when he visited Hereford. Innkeepers were aware of the opportunities, and when a new licensee took over it was quite common for a house-warming dinner to be held, often a few months after the licensee had taken over. John Jackson had a house-warming dinner when he took the Waterloo Hotel in Leominster in 1839. In 1843 he moved on to the Royal Oak, where he held regular dinners, such as farmers' and tradesmen's dinners, and in common with the other larger inns, sales by auction were regularly held. When John Jackson left the Royal Oak in 1856 there was also a farewell dinner.

Licensed premises have always been subject to much troublesome legislation. For many years it was the law that each licensee had to find, annually, two respectable persons to act as sureties that the licensee would conduct his business in a proper manner. This requirement was done away with by an Act of 1828, but under the Act the licensee was bound to use the legal, stamped measures, not to adulterate his drinks, and not to permit drunkenness on his premises. Two years later, during the premiership of the Duke of Wellington, the Beerhouse Act enabled those who wished to open a simple beer-house – no spirits – to do so by paying 2 guineas for an excise licence. Within twelve months about 24,000 had been opened across the country, to the dismay of some responsible employers. In Hereford a directory of 1835 listed a total of fifty inns, hotels, taverns and public houses, together with twenty-eight retailers of beer and cider, indicating the growth in licensed premises. John Benbow, a glove manufacturer in a large business in Hereford, in March 1831 published a letter in the *Hereford Journal* regarding his concern about the increase in over-indulgence in beer among his workforce. His letter was taken up in the editorial, which commented on it as 'one instance amongst many others that have been communicated to us, of the evils the Beer Act is inflicting on the working classes of this community'.

Acts of 1834 and 1840 followed – the first of these differentiated between 'on' and 'off' licences and made 'on' licences more difficult to obtain, whilst the second ensured that licences were issued only to the occupier of the premises. The complex legislation about licensed premises was tidied up with an Act of 1872, amended in 1874. Under these, there was a requirement for the magistrates to keep a register of licences and such lists are very useful for the historian. Regrettably, for Herefordshire very few survive.

Another piece of legislation that affected the county in a beneficial way was the Act of 1881 which banned Sunday drinking in Wales. However, liquid refreshment could be supplied at any time to *bona fide* travellers (defined as travelling over three miles), or to residents of the licensed premises. For those living just outside Herefordshire, rather than travel three miles it was easiest just to pop into Herefordshire for a drink on a Sunday, and places such as the Rhydspence benefitted. The 1961 Act, amended in 1964, allowed for polls to take place in the various administrative districts, and Wales gradually became 'wet' on a Sunday, beginning with those districts closest to England.

At the time of the Beer-house Acts there was little restriction on opening hours of licensed premises. While beer-houses had limited hours, from 4 a.m. to 10 p.m., with local variations, for other licensed premises the only non-permitted hours were during the times of Divine Services on Sundays, Christmas Day and Good Friday. At the end of the nineteenth century, they could still open for some twenty hours per day. During the First World War limited hours were introduced so that there would not be an adverse effect on the war effort, but also to discourage soldiers from drinking. In view of what the troops had to go through, this all seems very hard.

The Licensing Act of 1921 defined permitted hours as being between 11 a.m. and 10 p.m. except for Sundays, which were limited to five hours. During the century there were minor modifications to these hours, but with the new millennium twenty-four hour drinking is possible, under the 2003 Licensing Act.

Allusion has been made above to most inns brewing their own ale or beer. However, by the 1770s there was a brewery in the parish of Fownhope, on the road between Mordiford and Fownhope. This was run by Nathaniel Purchas in partnership with Robert Whittlesey until the latter's death in 1775, and the firm also acted as dealers in spirits. Their products were distributed over-land by teams of horses – one team in 1780 had a close escape from being struck by lightning – and by barge on the river Wye. Subsequently there was a spin-off from the brewery in that Thomas Purchas opened a wine and spirit merchant's business in Ross. Nathaniel Purchas died in 1817 and his son William carried on the brewing business. In 1827 he went into partnership with two others, the firm becoming 'Reynolds, Purchas and Reynolds'. In January 1829 William Purchas dropped out of the partnership, and in 1834 the brewery was moved to new, purpose-built premises in Bewell Street, Hereford. By 1839 the firm had become Reynolds & Wase, but closed in 1842, the sale details for the premises stating that the brewery was capable of producing 5,000 barrels of ale and porter annually.

Subsequently it appears that the buildings were left empty for a number of years before being taken over by Charles Watkins in 1858. He had come to Hereford some years previously, first at the Three Crowns, Eign Street, and then to the Imperial, Widemarsh Street, where he opened a small brewery – a business he expanded in the Bewell Street premises.

After Charles Watkins' death in 1889, the firm was run by his two surviving sons, Charles and Alfred, but the business empire, which by this time consisted not only of the brewery but a chain of thirty-five public houses and hotels, was sold in 1898. The business was acquired by the Tredegar Brewery Company, and in 1906 the Bewell Street site became the main production centre. After the Second World War there was a merger with the other brewery in Hereford. This was in Maylord Street, and was founded in the second half of the nineteenth century, becoming the City Brewery, which, in 1890, was bought by Arnold, Perrett & Co. of Wickwar, Gloucestershire. In 1924 the ownership of the Maylord Street premises was transferred to the Cheltenham Original Brewery Ltd. After the Second World War, the Cheltenham Original Brewery took over its competitor in Bewell Street, becoming the Cheltenham & Hereford Brewery Ltd. The Maylord Street site was sold off in 1951. In 1958 the Stroud Brewery Co. joined with the Cheltenham & Hereford Brewery to become the West Country Brewery. In 1963 Whitbreads bought the firm, brewing ceased, and all the buildings, with the exception of Bewell House, were demolished.

Finally, a word should be said about commercial production of cider. Late in the nineteenth and during the first half of the twentieth centuries, cider was made by several firms in Hereford including W. Evans and Co., H. Godwin & Son, and H.P. Bulmer & Co. In 1892, William Evans and Co.'s Cider Works were said to produce 'two favourite beverages, namely cider and perry, in greater perfection than any other town in England'. The sole proprietor, Mr W.F. Chave, was also Mayor of Hereford at that time. His works, in comparison to the farmhouse cider mills, were 'equipped with highly-improved modern machinery and labour-saving appliances, which enable the work to be done in a cleanly, efficient and economical manner'. Evans & Co. had their works on Widemarsh Common. They continued to produce cider in Hereford until well after the end of the Second World War, but eventually closed and the buildings had all been demolished by 1975. Godwin & Son had premises at Holmer, where their factory was enlarged and remodelled in 1913, but they too have been closed for many years.

Bulmer's was founded in 1887 by the sons of the rector of Credenhill, and by the following year the venture had prospered to such an extent that the business had moved to premises in Maylord Street. Operations were eventually centred in Ryelands Street and, more recently, in Plough Lane. Bulmer's were the largest cider producer in the country but were recently taken over by the Scottish & Newcastle Brewery.

While most of the larger producers were in the city of Hereford, there was a cider works at Manor Farm, Clehonger. In 1902 Richard Henry Ridler was farming here, but within a few years he started making cider on a commercial basis, an early example of diversification. The firm subsequently became Ridler & Son Ltd. and this was run in conjunction with the farming business. After the Second World War the firm became Evans & Ridler Ltd, but it closed in 1950 and the buildings were used for an engineering business.

Also in the country is the well-known firm of H. Weston and Sons, Ltd. In 1878 Henry Weston started farming at The Bounds, Much Marcle, making cider and perry from fruit grown on the farm. At that time agriculture was in a depressed state, and in 1880 he decided to make cider and perry as a commercial enterprise. He prospered, and gradually mechanised the process, but his full plans were only implemented after his death in 1917. The business has continued to expand ever since, and is still family-owned, with a widespread reputation.

John Eisel
Ron Shoesmith
June 2009

1

HEREFORD

The Greyhound Dog, Belmont Road, in its better days. The site is now lost under the Asda development.

In the nineteenth century Broad Street was, as now, a busy place, although the traffic moved at a much slower pace. A surprising number of places offering liquid refreshment can be seen on this print of 1847. The left-hand side starts with the Half Moon, then some four doors along and probably the building with the hanging lanterns, is the Green Dragon. Beyond, the twin gables of the White Hart can be seen, with the adjoining Nag's Head and the King's Head on the sides of West Street. On the right-hand side the cast iron balcony of the Mitre is prominent, with the triple gables of the White Swan beyond. Further on, but not visible, are the Queen's Head and the City Arms. Most of these are now closed, and the only ones of these establishments now open are a slightly extended Queen's Head, and the very much extended Green Dragon.

Opposite above: The Green Dragon is now the largest hotel in Hereford, its size belying its relatively humble origins. Initially being no larger than any other inn in the street, it has expanded even more since this photograph was taken at the beginning of the twentieth century. It was formerly one of the properties owned by the College of Vicars Choral, and its documented history starts in 1644 when it was called the White Lion and leased to one Barnabe Smyth, a baker. The annual rent was £3 5s and a couple of fat capons. The name was changed in or before 1708 as a twenty-nine year lease granted in that year stated that the property was called the 'Green Dragon formerly the White Lion'. In the late eighteenth century the Green Dragon became an important coaching inn, serving as a starting point not only for stage coaches to and from London, but acting as a connecting point where travellers from London on *Pruen's Flying Machine* could transfer to a diligence for Kington.

Early in the next century the Green Dragon was run by John Bosley, whose house-warming dinner was advertised in 1823. It rapidly improved under the capable hands of father John, followed by his sons, William and John. Between them they managed both the Green Dragon and the City Arms. The family also held the contract for conveying convicts to the 'hulks', and in 1824 was informed that no additional charge would be allowed beyond that due to them for using the most direct route! In the 1830s there was a coaching office at the Green Dragon with the Royal Mail leaving there daily at 2.15 p.m., and the *Champion* every day at 10 a.m. on their different routes to London.

In 1832 a hamper was discovered in the Green Dragon Coaching Office, which, because of suspicious circumstances, was opened and found to contain the body of an old man. It was proved to have been stolen from All Saints' burial ground. For this, two men were tried and sentenced to four months in custody, in addition to two months that they had already served. This lenient sentence caused much local resentment.

In 1843 the younger Bosley bought the Green Dragon, and a large assembly room was built. Then, in 1858, the present fine Italianate front was constructed (opposite). The expansion continued in 1863 with the acquisition of land on the opposite side of Aubrey Street on which new stabling was erected. In the twentieth century part of this was rented out to James Fryer, who built one of the earliest garages in Hereford, the ownership reverting to the Green Dragon in 1968 when the lease expired.

In 1928 the Green Dragon was refurbished, and expanded then again in 1930 by the acquisition of two buildings to the north, which were redeveloped and the classical front extended.

On the outbreak of war in 1939 the hotel was requisitioned at short notice, the cellars were bricked up, and a telephone was installed in every room. It was intended that it should be used as Government offices, but this was not pursued and it was used as a billet by the armed forces. It was handed back to the owners in 1946, ready for the Three Choirs Festival.

Nowadays, the Green Dragon provides a degree of elegance to the central part of Broad Street, an elegance that is sadly lacking further south where the glass and concrete 1960s buildings are a poor substitute to the variety of buildings that previously graced this part of the street.

Right: Facilities offered by the Green Dragon in 1867.

Prominent on the east side of Broad Street, opposite the Green Dragon and readily identifiable by its fine cast iron portico, was the Mitre Hotel, seen here in a photograph taken before the First World War. This property was also part of the endowments of the cathedral, and deeds prove that it was formerly called the Golden Lion, a name it may well have had in the seventeenth century. Thus the Golden Lion and the White Lion stood opposite one another. The name changed to the Mitre between 1774 and 1789, rather later than the name change of the Green Dragon.

About the year 1805 the present building was built, at a cost of approximately £670. During the earlier part of the nineteenth century there was a hanging balcony across the southern part of the façade, including the driving way, but no portico. Sometime after 1863 the balcony was removed and the present cast iron portico erected. It seems that the old balustrade was reused to form the present one. This was a convenient place from which to address any assembled crowds, and was used for this purpose in 1951 when the then Foreign Secretary, Anthony Eden, addressed a Broad Street crowd some 1,000 strong.

By 1892 the proprietresses, the Misses A. & M. Williams, were advertising that the Mitre had been appointed as a local headquarters for the Cyclists' Touring Club, although the enamel sign which must have been displayed is no longer there. This was the heyday of the cyclist, before the advent of the motor car, a change reflected in the early twentieth century fascia board which read 'Mitre Hotel, Stables and Garage' and there was, and still is, a wide driveway leading into the rear yard.

In the twentieth century the accommodation was mainly residential, and in 1921 the thriller writer Edgar Wallace stayed there during the famous nine-day trial of the Hay solicitor, Herbert Rowse Armstrong, for the murder of his wife. In a later thriller, Wallace referred to the Mitre as having a good cellar of port! Another regular visitor, famed for his portrayal of Long John Silver in the classic version of the film *Treasure Island*, was actor Robert Newton.

The final lease came to an end in 1955 and the Mitre closed to customers on 28 September, to become a bank. It is now the offices of a firm of solicitors.

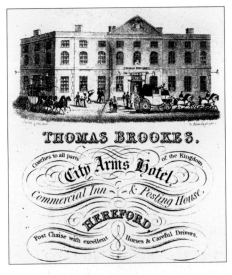

At the top of Broad Street was formerly the City Arms, seen here in a print of around 1830 but now recognisable as what is now Barclays bank. In 1549 it was called the 'Fawcon' and by the time of the Civil War it was known as the Swan and Falcon, a name it retained until the end of the eighteenth century. This was the most notable hotel in Hereford, and also a centre for stage-coaches. At this period the building projected well into the street, reflecting the Saxon north gate into the city, but causing an impediment to traffic. The present building was constructed as a town house for Charles Howard, 11th Duke of Norfolk, the foundation stone being laid early in 1791 and the completed building was opened on 9 July 1793. The name was changed to the City Arms in the summer of 1795. On the first floor was the Great Room, 70ft long and 28ft high, where many notable events took place. On 23 August 1802 there was a reception here for Admiral Lord Nelson, who was on a grand tour, accompanied by his mistress Lady Hamilton and her husband. Such was the pre-eminence of the City Arms that in the first half of the nineteenth century it was often just referred to as the 'Hotel'.

From the late eighteenth century to the arrival of the railways, the City Arms was a major coaching inn, with connections to many parts of the country. With the opening of the various railways from 1853 onwards there was a severe decline in the coaching trade, and the City Arms suffered accordingly. Probably because of this, in 1866 the northern part of the building was sold to a bank. This part was rebuilt, spoiling the symmetry of the Georgian façade. It is now a branch of Burtons. The City Arms recovered from its decline and in 1898 an additional block containing some twenty bedrooms was constructed to the rear, facing onto East Street. Late in 1927 the City Arms was sold, and the furniture followed in January 1928. Subsequently the hotel became part of the Trust House Group and it was renovated in 1939. Despite this, by the 1960s the foundations of the hotel, laid in the mud of the Saxon city ditch, began to move again. In 1973 planning permission was given to convert it into a branch of Barclays bank and the building was totally gutted leaving only the façade and part of the rear premises; a new building was then built within the shell. The old back bar still survives however, although well hidden, in which one of the authors celebrated the end of his schooldays, not wisely but too well!

GENERAL COACH OFFICE,
CITY ARMS HOTEL, HEREFORD.

THE following MAILS and LIGHT POST COACHES leave the above Office:—

London ROYAL MAIL, through Cheltenham every Evening at Half past Two.

Chester and Liverpool ROYAL MAIL every Morning at Half past Five.

Shrewsbury and Holyhead ROYAL MAIL every Morning at Half past Five.

London TELEGRAPH LIGHT COACH, Four inside, every Morning, Sunday excepted, at Half past Ten, through Worcester and Oxford, to Griffins Green Man, Oxford-street, and the Bull and-Mouth, Bull-and-Mouth-street, by 7 the following Morning.

London LIGHT COACH, THE CAMBRIAN, every Tuesday, Thursday, and Saturday Evening, at Five o'clock, to the Crown Inn, Worcester, leaves Worcester every Morning at Six o'clock, and arrives at Griffin's Green Man, Oxford-street, and the Bull-and-Mouth, Bull-and-Mouth-street, by Seven the same Evening.

Worcester, Birmingham, Wolverhampton, Coventry, and Manchester LIGHT COACH, Four inside, every Morning, except Ten.

CAMBRIAN LIGHT COACH, through Brecon and Carmarthen to Tenby, Haverfordwest, and Milford, every Monday, Wednesday, and Friday Mornings at Ten, where it will meet the Steam Packets for Ireland.

TELEGRAPH LIGHT COACH to Hay and Brecon every Tuesday, Thursday, and Saturday Evening, at Half past Two, where it will meet Coaches for Merthyr Tydvil, Neath, and Swansea; also Builth, Llandrindod Wells, and Newtown.

Performed by JAMES BENNETT & Co.

Who will not be accountable for any Parcel or Package above the Value of Five Pounds, unless entered as such, and an Insurance paid above the common Carriage.

In the eighteenth century there was an inn called the Spread Eagle on the north bank of the river, built against the east side of the Wye Bridge. It was certainly still called by this name at the end of the eighteenth century, but the building was demolished when the bridge was widened in the 1820s. Hence it must not be confused with the present Spread Eagle in King Street. This is in a building that dates from the early seventeenth century, but which is built on a late medieval cellar. It still has its driveway, now used as a sitting-out area. Despite assumptions of antiquity, the first certain mention of this pub is in a directory of 1850. In the latter part of the century, like many Hereford pubs, this was a carriers' base. In the 1920s the stables were still in regular use and could accommodate up to seventy-two horses. Not only that, in 1948 they were used to house a circus that visited Hereford, including some lions! In the 1960s and 1970s Frank's Steak Bar was a feature of the Spread Eagle, remembered with nostalgia by many Herefordians. There have been relatively recent changes to the interior, although the division of the rooms on either side of the stairwell is preserved.

The Orange Tree in King Street, a building dating from the early seventeenth century, was re-fronted in brick in the middle of the nineteenth century. What it looked like then can be seen behind this jolly party. Formerly belonging to the Hereford Brewery, it was sold in 1898 and the new owners, the Hereford & Tredegar Brewery Ltd, had it re-fronted again in 1907. This front survived when the roof and upper floor of the inn were badly damaged by fire in April 1994, pictured here being damped down, when much water damage was also caused. A careful restoration took some months to complete, and the opportunity was taken to build an extension to the rear. At the beginning of the new millennium the internal open interior was refurbished, carefully retaining the original panelling on the east wall and the few remaining timbers of the rear wall. Thus, despite the renovations, the interior preserves much of its old character. Since then history has repeated itself, and the Orange Tree has now reopened after another fire. (Above: Derek Foxton Collection)

Left: The Black Lion, Bridge Street, during alterations in 1910.

Below: The drab face of the Black Lion as it appeared between the two world wars. (Derek Foxton Collection)

The only inn still operating in Bridge Street is the historic Black Lion, one of the oldest inns in Hereford to survive to the present day. But it has suffered many alterations since it was built. The main part of the building dates back to the middle or second half of the sixteenth century, with slightly later additions to front and rear.

The Black Lion had been in use as an inn for many years when, in July 1778, there was the following advertisement, 'To be sold. A messuage or tenement known by the sign of the Black Lion, being a well-accustomed Inn situate in Wyebridge Street, in the occupation of Thomas Drew, with the garden, stables and Brewhouse'. The grounds were relatively long and narrow and stretched back as far as the City Wall, which formed its western boundary. The various outhouses associated with the inn

were, and still are, in a long row against the northern boundary. The southern boundary of the plot was also the parish boundary separating St Nicholas parish to the north from St John's parish to the south.

In earlier times the access to the inn yard to the rear was through a driveway under the left-hand part of the present building (opposite top), but very late in the nineteenth century or early in the following one, the narrow property to the south of the parish boundary was added to the Black Lion establishment. Radical alterations took place in 1910 when the new southern property was completely demolished to provide a new and wider access to the yard. The old driveway was then blocked up, windows were inserted and it is now part of the bar. Whilst the conversion work was in progress, the historic timberwork on the front elevation was exposed to view for a short period, but at that time it was not considered attractive and was once again covered with render (opposite).

In a room on the first floor of the inn are the remains of a series of wall paintings, representing people breaking the Ten Commandments, which were discovered in 1932. It is not suggested that these represent the landlord or his customers! It is suggested, however, that they may have been painted by John Gildon, who carved several tombs in the area in the late sixteenth century.

In the period between the two world wars, the house was always known as the Black Lion Agricultural Inn and had a rather forbidding exterior, rendered and lined to look like stone.

The inn sign was just the simple name with, perhaps slightly more encouragingly underneath it 'Excellent garage for charsabanc (*sic*), motors etc'. The present Black Lion has succeeded in gaining a much more friendly appearance since the render was removed, once again exposing the seventeenth-century timber framework that is such a feature of this building (above).

One of the sights of Hereford is the old Wye Bridge which, when it was built around 1490, had a gateway at the southern end. After damage in the seventeenth-century Civil War, the remains were finally demolished in 1782. The bridge was widened in the 1820s and carried all the traffic crossing the Wye until the Greyfriars Bridge was built in 1967.

One historic inn has survived all these changes, the Saracen's Head, although with some slight variations in name from time to time. For a short while it was called the Lancaster to commemorate the well-known bomber of Second World War fame, but has now reverted to the name by which it has been known for hundreds of years – the Saracen's Head. It is on the downstream side of the bridge, just opposite where the gate used to stand, and surviving deeds relating to this property go back to 1359.

From its position, the Saracen's Head (seen above in a 1994 photograph) was one of the inns associated with the river trade, and buildings from this phase of Hereford's history still survive downstream from the inn. While the landlord no doubt profited from the river trade, relations were not always good and in January 1796 complaints were made by the various bargemasters of obstructions caused by Mr Grundy, the occupier of the Saracen's Head. All this trade diminished after the arrival of the South Wales tramway in 1826, and completely finished after the railways arrived in Hereford in the 1850s. At the time of the complaint it is known that the inn extended right up to the river bank. Once the wharves fell out of use the corporation, who owned the building, dismantled the north wall of the inn and rebuilt it further back in order to provide the pathway that still leads directly along the river bank. They paid the tenant compensation of £100 whilst the work was in progress.

The Saracen's Head must be one of the only inns to have two official names, although the second name, the City Arms, granted by the city magistrates, is used on just two days a year – 1st June and 1st December. This name is used in connection with the various Wye Navigation Acts, for the Acts state that meetings shall be held in the City Arms.

The historic Bunch of Grapes is the sole survivor of at least four inns that used to be in this part of Church Street (a part formerly known as Narrow Capuchin Lane). In the 1820s the official name was the Royal Oak and Grapes, but it was usually known just as the Grapes.

A feature of the inn in the nineteenth century was the reading room, the atmosphere of which was captured in the early 1990s photograph (above), where the news was read out as it was received in Hereford. The seats were allocated, and when the occupant of a seat died, a new occupant had to be elected!

Being built on the old Saxon ditch, the building, dating in the main from the seventeenth century, became unsafe and was closed in 1988. After a careful survey, the inn was carefully stabilised and restored, in 1994.

Because the elevation facing East Street was falling outwards, this had to be completely rebuilt (above right). Inevitably some of the character has been lost, but rather that than lose such an historic inn altogether. It is now a well cared for and attractive pub, which makes a positive contribution to the streetscape of this part of the city.

CITY OF HEREFORD

GRAPES TAVERN
One of the city's oldest inns,
dating from the early 17th century

THE LONDON LETTER
which was delivered weekly by
stage coach, was read here by
a chairman appointed
annually to the
office.

BOOTH HALL INN
HIGH TOWN
HEREFORD

RESTORATION
of OLD OAK ROOF
DISCOVERED IN JUNE 1919
DURING ALTERATIONS TO PREMISES

Herbert Skyrme M.S.A
Architect
Hereford

Hidden up a narrow passage leading from High Town to East Street is the Booth Hall, one of the most historic buildings and licensed premises in Hereford. In 1392 one citizen sold the 'Bothehall' to another, and then six months later, the Mayor and commonalty of Hereford obtained from the king a licence to acquire the building and grounds. The present building was built at some time in the second half of the fifteenth century. Its antiquity was appreciated in 1876 when a writer in the *Hereford Times* noted that 'although a great portion is very old I understand it has been well kept and in good repair'. The writer went on to recollect that in his youth 'many times hearing of a ghost that was said to have haunted it, and that it was positively laid by a visitation of dignitaries of the Cathedral and other clergymen and pious people and sundry laymen, several of whom were somewhat of the wag genus. I have heard the late facetious "Tom Cooke" describe the event, but I have now forgotten the particulars'.

The main part of the inn was the nineteenth century range of buildings fronting onto High Town, now used for other purposes, and the precise whereabouts of the Booth Hall itself was only rediscovered in 1919 when a chimney stack fell, exposing the magnificent medieval roof timbers. Also apparent was the poor state of the building, as seen in this photograph (right) taken during the restoration. Much timber had to be replaced and the results, on the opposite page, are dramatic, although a first floor was inserted.

The exact date when the Booth Hall first became an inn is uncertain. There was certainly a cockpit here in 1686 and when the sale by auction of the inn was advertised in the *Hereford Journal* in 1827 it was stated that it had been established for over 100 years, suggesting that it became an inn in the early eighteenth century. At that time it was in the hands of the Gwillim family, and in 1783 George Willim (*sic*) was allowed to buy the whole property from the city authorities providing he rebuilt the front to High Town 'in a handsome and ornamental manner'. Willim's building (Nos 18 and 19 High Town) still stands although it has had many alterations.

Tom Winter Spring, the notable pugilist, was landlord here in the early years of the nineteenth century. As a native of Fownhope, it must have been something of a homecoming when he became landlord in 1824. Not long after this he was attacked by six men who had refused to pay their score. This was a serious mistake on their part, and Spring laid all of them out on the floor, and then ejected them one at a time! Tom Spring left Hereford for the Castle Tavern, Holborn, London in 1827, holding his farewell dinner in Hereford on 6 December in that year.

At the beginning of the twentieth century the Booth Hall was well settled as a 'Commercial and Agricultural Hotel' serving 'the choicest wines, spirits, ales, and cigars' including 'Bass's Ales, Guinness's Stout and Pure Herefordshire Cider direct from the Maker'. G.A. Wigley was the proprietor and advertised his establishment as 'One of the oldest Licensed Houses in this Ancient City'. Accommodation was important and in 1939 when it had, rather inevitably, become Ye Olde Booth Hall it had thirteen rooms, all with hot and cold water, and in the Assembly Room seating for 150.

In September 2002 a proposal to insert a spiral stair from the bar below through the centre of the floor of the hall itself met with some local opposition, but permission was granted, and it is now possible to have a drink in the bar and view the fine ceiling through the stairwell.

In earlier times there were at least six licensed establishments in Church Street between High Town and the Cathedral Close. Of these the only survivor is the Lichfield Vaults which retains a prominent position on the east side of the street, pictured here in an early twentieth century photograph (above left). At an earlier date it was called the Dog Inn, and as such was mentioned in 1782 and 1799. In September in the latter year it was advertised as being to let 'That well-accustomed *Public-house* called the DOG, situate in Broad Capuchin-lane in the city...' In 1851, when James Morgan was in charge, it was described as the Old Dog. However, the Dog was not shown on the 1858 city map or mentioned in the directory for that year, so the licence may have lapsed for a while, but not for too long, as the Dog is mentioned in a directory of 1867. Whatever was happening at that time, the name change occurred about the year 1880, and this was probably due to a change of lessee, for in 1914, when alterations were proposed, the proprietors were given as 'The Lichfield Brewery Co. Ltd'.

Before the alterations took place, the ground floor plan consisted of a large 'L'-shaped smoke room towards the rear of the building, which was approached by a long side passage. It was very much a meeting room with wall seating and two fireplaces. At the front of the building was a minute public bar, about 8ft long by 5ft wide – smaller than a prison cell – and inevitably with standing room only. At that time the inn had a double gable to the front and the whole face had been rendered. The render was eventually removed to expose the original brick, but this was unsatisfactory and new ideas were sought.

The proposals were radical for 1914, as they envisaged one large room containing both bar and smoke room. Such a scheme may well have alienated the customers from both sides as a hand-written note was added to the plans to ensure that a screen was erected between the two parts. The proprieties were preserved and the separation between workmen and tradesmen was to continue at the Lichfield for another half-century. Even now there is still some separation between the front and rear public areas.

The extent of the alterations to the façade can be seen by comparing the earlier photograph with the other photograph (above right), taken in 2004. It is pleasing to be able to report that, after a period of closure, the Lichfield Vaults is once again dispensing excellent hospitality.

The only survivor of several pubs that were formerly in Bewell Street is the Bowling Green Inn. Behind it, the bowling green is claimed to be one of the oldest in the country, possibly laid out as early as 1484, but the first specific mention of the green as such is in 1697. In the eighteenth and early nineteenth centuries, when the bowling season was in full swing, a regular dinner was held at the Bowling Green.

In 1912 the renewal of the licence was challenged because of the poor state of the premises, the lack of maintenance being blamed by the owners (Messrs Flower & Sons, of Stratford) on planning blight caused by a proposal to widen the street. Accordingly, plans were prepared to rebuild the inn set back from the street, but progress was stopped by the First World War, and these plans were not implemented until the 1930s. However, the plans for a newer, wider, street never happened, leaving the new Bowling Green Inn with a forecourt which is now put to good use as a smoking area – a way that was never intended!

On the west side of Widemarsh Street, opposite Maylord Street, is the Imperial. Charles Watkins, the founder of the Imperial Brewery, moved here in the late 1840s and started his brewery at the rear of the premises, later expanding into premises in Bewell Street. At this period the Imperial was a long, narrow, building. The adjacent building on the north side was rebuilt in 1857 as the Albion Hotel, much larger than the Imperial, was sold off in 1898, in 1900 the Imperial and the Albion Hotel, were combined into a single building by a reconstruction of the front portion. This much-admired example of vernacular revivalism was opened on 28 June 1901. The division between the old Imperial and the Albion Hotel can still be seen in the façade of the building in the 1930s view. (Derek Foxton Collection)

No. 7.

THE "IMPERIAL VAULTS,"

No. 12. Widemarsh Street, Hereford.

An important FULLY-LICENSED PROPERTY, situate adjoining the "Old Mansion House," and present Municipal Buildings, also opposite the General Markets belonging to the Corporation,

AND CONTAINING

Large Bar with four Entrances, Smoke Room, Kitchen, Back Kitchen, large Sitting Room, Spirit Room, Two Bed Rooms, Stock Room and Cellar in Basement. Long Yard with old Brewhouse used as Cellars, and Sheds beyond.

Under Management; but of the estimated Rental Value of **£80 per Annum.**

ALSO

THE SHOP AND PREMISES ADJOINING,

BEING

No. 13, Widemarsh Street, Hereford.

FORMERLY LICENSED AS "THE ALBION,"

AND CONTAINING

On GROUND FLOOR—Spacious Shop, large Stock Room, Parlour, Kitchen and Back Kitchen.   On FIRST FLOOR—Large Show Room, Sitting Room and W.C., Housemaids' Closet and Sink.   On SECOND FLOOR—Six Bed Rooms. In BASEMENT—Two large Cellars used by the "Imperial Vaults."   In the REAR—Yard and Garden.

Let temporarily to Messrs. C. Robertson & Co., Complete House Furnishers, at a Rent of **£1 : 10 : 0 per Week,** the Brewery paying Rates and Taxes.

FREEHOLD.

Looking northwards from the west end of High Town along Widemarsh Street, the vista was formerly closed at the north end by the town gate, demolished in 1798. To the east of the gate is a substantial building dating from the early seventeenth century, which is now the Farmers' Club and licensed, although as a private club (above).

On the west side of the gate was a licensed premises which was partly built over the city wall. This seems to have been the Black Boy, but at the time of the painting was called the Harp, a name changed to the Volunteer and then the Wellington Arms. It is now JDs.

The inn was bought by the City Council in 1876, which sold it on (with stringent conditions) in 1891, after which the old inn was demolished and the present building erected. To do this, part of the old city wall had to be demolished, the whole being replaced by the present brick building.

Left: The rebuilt Wellington Inn. (Derek Foxton Collection)

Above: In the late eighteenth and early nineteenth centuries Hereford cattle market was held in Broad Street and the sheep and pig market in the parallel Wroughtall, now Aubrey Street. To remedy the situation, under the Hereford Improvement Act of 1854, a new market site on the north-west of the town ditch was bought for £2,500. The sale included a house that had been built in 1812, which was used for a short while as the Hereford Improvement Office. During the construction of the market, the present New Market Street was laid out. It is not surprising that the Improvement Office became the New Market Tavern, then the Cattle Market Inn. William Simpson was the first proprietor, and the inn was described in 1858 in the following terms, 'At the entrance from Widemarsh-street is a handsome and commodious inn, attached to which is a large room, suitable for public meetings, exhibitions, balls, concerts &c., &c.;'

On 13 October 1857 William Simpson held a house-warming dinner in the 'large room' referred to above. This was about 55ft by 22ft, but at the opening there were complaints that there was insufficient height. William Simpson issued a fine engraved publicity card, illustrated above, in which he featured this concert room.

Being set well back from the road in its acre of grounds, the Tavern was not affected by the construction of the inner relief road, during which New Market Street was widened. In 2008 it was refurbished and reopened as the Old Market Inn, and it still continues to serve visitors to the market as it has for 150 years. The name reflects the possible move to a position north of the city in which case the inn may be the only reflection of this busy area of Hereford in the late nineteenth and twentieth centuries.

Opposite above: The Merton Hotel in 1908. (Derek Foxton Collection)

The Merton Hotel is next to the entrance that leads into the disused St Peter's burial ground, almost opposite the site of the former county gaol. It shared its name with Merton Passage, a terrace of small houses that ran at right angles to Commercial Road in the nineteenth and early twentieth centuries. Probably built as a private house early in the nineteenth century, it seems to have been opened as a hotel by Charles Farr about 1863. He also operated a funeral business, an 1891 advert for which is illustrated below.

Farr died in the early 1890s and by 1896 his widow decided to retire, and put the whole establishment up for sale by auction. Besides the hotel it included the nine cottages in Merton Passage and the four houses between the Merton and St Peter's Burial Ground. At that time the hotel had twelve bedrooms, and its status was assured by the provision of hot and cold shower-baths at all times. At the rear of the hotel were two assembly rooms approached by a covered way from the main part of the building.

The houses next to the Merton Hotel and the cottages at the rear have long since disappeared. The hotel has expanded along the frontage and is now a free house. Between the hotel and the graveyard there is the obligatory smoking area!

FUNERALS FURNISHED.

MERTON ✤ HOTEL

AND

General Posting House,

COMMERCIAL ROAD, HEREFORD,

(Within 3 minutes' walk of Railway Station.)

CHARLES FARR, Proprietor.

Saddle Horses, Dog Carts, Brakes, Flys, Landaus, Broughams, Private Carriages, &c., always on Hire by Day or Week. Loose Boxes & Lock-up Coach Houses.

MERTON OMNIBUS TO AND FROM THE RAILWAY STATION.

THIS HEARSE WITH EITHER GLASS SIDES OR CARVED PANELS.

Hot and Cold Shower Baths always ready at the Hotel.

St Owen's Street was one of the main roads into the city from the east, access being gained through St Owen's Gate. Just outside the site of the gate, built on the old city ditch, was the Lamb (above left). This is an inn of some antiquity and was another property that was owned by the city. In the eighteenth century the annual rent was 6s 8d, but when the lease was renewed the entry fine varied from £13 upwards for a twenty-one year term. In the 1820s the name was given as the Lamb and Flag, which would appear to have been the official name. The city authorities subsequently sold the inn, and it was held from about 1838 by George Russell, who offered it for sale ten years later. It was sold again in 1906 when it was bought by Ind Coope.

The Lamb became the Barrels in 1987 and is the home of the Wye Valley Brewery. Because of the success of that concern, brewing was transferred to the former Symonds cider works at Stoke Lacy in 2002. In this modern photograph both names can be clearly seen, the former name being in relief in the render above the entrance.

The Shire Hall is one of the most prominent landmarks of Hereford, built on the site of the former county gaol. Adjoining it on the St Owen's Street side is the Fleece (above right), replacing an earlier Fleece that was burnt down in December 1787. A report on the county gaol, published in 1790, complained that there was 'an improper means of communication between the Keeper's house and an adjoining house' allowing the introduction of 'spirituous liquors' into the gaol. In July 1804 it was ordered that the offending window be stopped up. This was not at all satisfactory to Mrs Sylvester, the landlady of the Fleece, and she stood up for her rights. As a result, a compromise was effected at the next Sessions so that she could keep the window open, but had to sign an acknowledgment that this was by agreement of Sessions, and that no liquor could pass through the window!

By 1870 it had brightened up to become the Golden Fleece, a name that was to stay with it to the present day. A very long and narrow building, the two small drinking rooms and the narrow passage that formerly led through the building to the rear yard have all been amalgamated into one large room, but the thinness of the plot – doubtless one of the burgage plots laid out by William Fitz Osbern for his French settlers over 900 years ago – is still apparent.

2

LEOMINSTER AND ITS VICINITY

The Greyhound, Rainbow Street, Leominster, in
1999 shortly before it closed. An Oddfellows Hall
was built here in 1838.

With a recorded history going back to the seventh century, Leominster is second in size only to Hereford. Such was its importance that from 1297 it sent two members to Parliament, although with a very limited franchise not extended until after the Reform Act of 1832. Another Reform Act of 1867 deprived Leominster of one of its members, and after an Act of 1885 the borough was merged with the county. Part of the reason for Leominster's importance in earlier times was its position on a crossroads, where the main road from Hereford to Ludlow and Shrewsbury – important strategic places in the turbulent Welsh Marches – crossed the road from Worcester into central Wales, a route that became more important as times became more settled. With peace comes prosperity, and Leominster benefited from being a market town, with buildings such as the former Market Hall, built by John Abel in 1633. There was a need for places where those trading in the markets could stable their horses, gain refreshment (both solid and liquid) and do business. Thus, like all market towns, Leominster had more licensed premises than the population could support in the ordinary way of things.

In 1675 John Ogilby published an atlas of road maps, each in strip form, one of which described the road from Hereford to Ludlow. One of the landmarks on the southern outskirts of Leominster was the Flower de Luce Inn, the only inn that it marked in Leominster, although there must have been many others. Nothing further is known of the Flower de Luce, but it must have been in the vicinity of the present Black Horse whose earlier name was the Bowling Green Inn. Up to the beginning of the nineteenth century the only bowling green in the town was behind the Unicorn in Broad Street but this closed in 1801, and the first certain mention of the Bowling Green Inn in South Street comes in 1826, when the name of Charles Howis is given in a Poll List. Charles Thomas, a later licensee, was here by 1863 and still resident in 1895, so evidently he found the position congenial. The name change to the Black Horse is a post-war phenomenon. The photograph below was taken in 1999.

Although a licensed establishment named the Royal Oak was in existence in the early eighteenth century, this was in a different site and so far the present Royal Oak cannot be traced earlier than a Poll List of 1802. Always very prominent in the life of the town, a large assembly room was added to the facilities by Thomas Corfield, the then proprietor, and opened with a public dinner in October 1837. In December of that year Corfield advertised that he had 'completed extensive additions to his house'.

When the Royal Oak was auctioned in August 1888 it was described in the following terms. 'The ROYAL OAK HOTEL, now in the occupation of Mr George Bedford, at the yearly annual rental of £270, but formerly, for many years, in that of the late owner, Mr John Bradford, and previously in that of the late Mr John Jackson, during whose management the Oak has had a wide-spread reputation as a first-class Family, Commercial, and Posting House, situated in the centre of the town, five minutes walk from Railway Station and Post Office, has a frontage of 97 feet to South-street and 166 feet to Etnam-street, Leominster'. While little has changed on the outside, the Royal Oak now offers accommodation for corporate functions and weddings, and even has an internet café, but it still retains an open fire in the bar.

Left: The Talbot in the 1930s.

Below: The first floor landing and sitting room in the Talbot in the 1930s.

While this 1930s photograph of the Talbot, West Street (opposite above), seems to indicate that it is just an ordinary inn, the truth is that it has since absorbed the adjacent properties so as to compete in size with the Royal Oak, occupying the whole corner of West and South Streets. It was evidently of some status in the eighteenth century, as a friendly society was established there in 1753, the rules of which were revised in 1822. In the early 1790s the proprietor was John Bradford, a saddler as well as an innkeeper, and despite several attempts to sell it, the family held the lease until well into the next century. In 1794 the Talbot was offered for sale by auction, the advertisement stating that the 'great part whereof is newly built'.

William Davis, who took over the tenancy in January 1795, was there until 1805, when he announced that he had bought the King's Arms, Leominster, and that the Talbot was to become a private house. This was incorrect and clearly he hoped to take his clientele with him! Samuel Burt took over the Talbot in 1808, paying an annual rent of £30. He evidently prospered, for in 1813 Burt moved on to the Royal Oak. Mr & Mrs Lucas, licensees from 1864, made the opposite move, for they had previously acted as servants to John Jackson, who was the successful proprietor of the Royal Oak from late 1842 until the 1850s. After her husband's death in 1881, Mrs Lucas carried on for another ten years, and must have been a sitting tenant when the Talbot was sold in 1890 for £1,525. By 1900 the Talbot was being run by Mrs Kate Annie Burton, who owned the premises, and she was there until the late 1930s. The two photographs illustrated here were taken in the 1930s, and show the first floor (opposite below) and the bar (below). At that period the inn occupied Nos 5 and 7 West Street, and Mrs Burton also owned the Talbot Vaults, just round the corner in South Street, formerly the King's Head. Since the Second World War Nos 1, 3 and 9 West Street have also been integrated into the Talbot to form the present hotel.

The Grapes, in Broad Street, is a pleasant, old-style hostelry with an interesting history.

In the 1840s it was run by William Cartwright, a wine and spirit merchant, whose grandson, Thomas Smith, lived with him. After his marriage in 1850, Thomas took over the business but soon slipped back into a life of drunkenness, from which he was saved when he saw the light. Wishing to do the same for others, he became secretary to a local mission, and also wrote the story of his life, entitled *A Brand Plucked from the Burning*, as a warning to others. Finding that running a wine merchant's business did not sit easily with his conscience, in 1855 he sold it to John Langford, who ran it for many years, followed by William Spooner Langford. In 1903 W.S. Langford was recorded as the owner and occupier of the Grapes. In the early years of the twentieth century, when it was being run by Mrs Susannah Weaver, it was described as a public house, rather than a wine merchants.

Left: A recent convivial scene at the Grapes

The name over the entry and the lion sitting on the parapet of this building on the west side of Broad Street are clues that this was formerly the Red Lion Inn, later the Lion Hotel. After the death of Mrs Morris, landlady of the inn in 1779, it was taken over by Henry Taylor and its rise to prominence began. In 1798 he advertised that he 'has fitted up and furnished his Dwelling-house in the neatest stile, and at a considerable expence...'. In 1804 Henry Taylor retired from the Red Lion to follow the trade of a skinner, and the licence was taken over by George Scoble. At that time the meetings of the Leominster Turnpike Trust and the Leominster Assembly were both held there. It was described in an 1808 guide in the following terms 'The Red Lion, in Broad street, which lets post-chaises and horses, and where the Hereford and Shrewsbury stage-coach stops for refreshment; the Excise-office is also kept here; it is a well-built brick building, and commodious for travellers. Landlord, Mr Scoble'. George Scoble held the Red Lion until his death in 1811, and the following year his widow married William Barrett, who ran the Red Lion until 1814. Barrett moved to Tenbury and in 1819 was imprisoned for debt in Worcester gaol.

After various licensees, in May 1843 the *Hereford Times* announced that the Lion Family and Commercial Hotel and Posting House had been entered by Thomas W. Prosser and had recently been rebuilt and very considerably enlarged. This referred to the building of the large Assembly Room at the rear of the premises. However the times were against this sort of enterprise, and after Prosser left in May 1847, the Lion Hotel was closed until George Devereux entered the premises more than a year later. But he didn't survive long, and in September 1848 he appeared in the Bankruptcy Court in Birmingham. In 1856 Mr J.G. Woodhouse, a local solicitor and the owner of the Lion, advertised the hotel as being to let, but it seems that there were no takers, and in 1860 the Lion was sold by auction. It subsequently became the premises of Samuel Alexander, ironmonger and agricultural implement maker, a firm that later became Alexander and Duncan, and the Assembly Room was used as display space, and then forgotten. It is only in recent years that it has been realised that it was substantially intact, and so was carefully restored, making a splendid meeting place and concert hall.

This 1970s view of the Three Horse Shoes in the Corn Market, Leominster, emphasises how it could benefit from its position. Built about the year 1600 it could have been an inn from the start. When the inn was advertised to be sold by auction in 1790, the second lot in the auction was three stables, close to the Three Horse Shoes, capable of holding eighteen or twenty horses. About 1806 Robert Trotter took over as landlord, being succeeded by his widow Theodosia and son (also Robert) in partnership, Robert junior on his own, and then daughter Harriet Trotter. The Three Horse Shoes was where Thomas Smith from the Grapes started his descent down the slippery slope of gambling and drinking, somewhere about the year 1847, just before the death of the younger Robert Trotter. When Harriet Trotter advertised the inn as being for sale or to let in 1849, the advert emphasized the good stabling that went with the inn, very necessary because of its position. Various landlords followed in the 1850s, and Edward Bird, who took over early in 1860, died in June that year, leaving his widow Susannah to run the inn and look after their eight children. She was still there in 1885, but was shortly succeeded by Tom Mitchell, who was also a manufacturer of aerated water. At the beginning of the twentieth century the Three Horse Shoes was owned by Alfred Molyneux, but the occupier was Elijah Molyneux. In recent years the name has become The Three Horseshoes, rather than its original form, and the sign, with its emblem of three horseshoes, has been replaced by one with only the most recent form of the name.

Above: The Three Horse Shoes in 2000.

Right: A bill for the Three Horse-shoes in 1771.

17th Sep.r 1771

THE

Three Horse-Shoes

IN

LEOMINSTER.

	£.	S.	D.
Eating - - - - - - - - - - - -			
Wine - - - - - - - - - - - -			
Punch - - - - - - - - - - - -	0	7	6
Coffee and Tea - - - - - - -			
Ale and Beer - - - - - - - -	0	6	4
Cyder - - - - - - - - - - - -			
Servants Eating and Ale - - - -			
Horses Hay and Corn - - - - - -			

Received ye Cont.t

£ y.r Coates

0 13 10

£1 7 2

£1 1 0

On the corner of Bridge Street and Mill Street, seen here in a recent photograph, the Hop Pole is the only survivor of several inns set around the junction. Nearby was the old Anchor Inn, closed in 1964 and demolished soon after for road widening, leaving the Hop Pole closer to the road junction than it was previously. Formerly leased from the borough of Leominster, in 1828 it was held by William Tanner and Thomas Tomkins, but a lease was taken out by John Jones in 1833, who had probably previously been a sub-tenant. Jones died in 1867, and when the inn was advertised to be let, it was stated that he had been the proprietor for forty-two years! He was a redoubtable character, and about the year 1830 was involved in fist fight with Tommy Dug. After this had been going on for an hour, Dr Taylor, a Justice of the Peace was sent for to stop the fight, but when the Justice arrived the spectators begged him not to interfere. So he stayed to watch for half an hour and then went home. The fight went on for another hour and a half, the reminiscence of the fight concluding 'I remember Jones's face was already a fearful sight when the doctor arrived, but he pluckily kept on and wore Tommy Dug out'.

For a short time around 1900 the licensee was Charles Henry Bastow, not too surprising as at that time the inn was owned by the Ledbury brewers Lane Bros & Bastow. In recent years the inn was closed for a while, but now has a new lease of life, with the covered entry at the side now put to use as a smoking shelter, a use that former publicans would never have thought of!

Just over the road from the Hop Pole, and easily identified by its ceramic Cheltenham & Hereford Breweries plaque, is the former Golden Lion Inn. Already an inn by 1780, until the middle of the nineteenth century there were only two landlords. The inter-war years were a prosperous time for the Golden Lion, particularly on Tuesdays and Fridays, the main market days, when the stables and yard were full. The inn was one of the premises affected by the regular floods in this part of Leominster, now thankfully a thing of the past as a result of drainage works in the early 1960s. Regretfully, it closed a number of years ago, and was used for a time as an antique shop.

The Bell in Etnam Street, seen here in a modern view, came into existence in the late 1820s, and no earlier name has been traced. In the past it has been confused with the earlier pub of the same name in Church Street, run by Samuel Nicholas the postmaster, which closed in the early 1820s. The first landlord of the later Bell to be traced was Benjamin Moss, and when he advertised it as being to let in 1830 it was said to be 'now in full business'. James Ovens, who took over in the late 1850s, held an annual pigeon shoot, no doubt to help business. After his death in the early 1860s the Bell was run briefly by one Benjamin Teague, before James's widow Charlotte took over again. She was still there in 1881. Another wife who took over from her husband was Eliza Dykes, who succeeded her husband William in 1902. At that time the Bell was owned by Allsopp's Brewery of Burton-on-Trent and sold Allsopp's Ales. Now the ales that are sold are local, and the pub hosts live music sessions.

In this early twentieth century view down Etnam Street the Chequers is immediately recognisable from its twin gables, but the adjacent building has long since disappeared. A long description of the building was given in 1934 by the Royal Commission on Historical Monuments, which stated that it was built around 1600. The inn is not mentioned in the *Universal British Directory* of 1793 and the first mention found is in a Poll List of 1796, when William Rogers was the innkeeper. He left in 1812 or just before, and was succeeded by Thomas Wilkes, who died in 1838, to be succeeded as licensee by his widow, Elizabeth.

After the death of Elizabeth Wilkes in 1856, the inn was taken over by James Biddle, who had been born in Ripple, Worcestershire but was then living in Leominster. Thus began a long and clearly successful connection of the Biddle family with the Chequers, where the family brewed their own ale. Not that this was unusual, as most innkeepers did, but in 1879 James was described as a retail brewer, indicating that he sold his products to other publicans. James retired from the Chequers in the late 1880s, and his son John Job Biddle took over both the pub and the brewing activities. This was a change in career, as in the 1881 census he was described as an unemployed engine fitter. In 1890, together with the Chequers, John Job Biddle was recorded as Superintendent and Engineer of the Leominster Fire Brigade, the engines of which were kept at the Fire Engine House in New Street. James Biddle died in retirement in 1893, and the ownership of the property passed to his widow Mary, so that in the 1903 list of licensed establishments, J.J. Biddle was recorded as the occupier, and Mary Biddle, then of Cardiff, the owner. J.J. Biddle kept the Chequers until about 1930 and was succeeded by Harold Job Biddle, who was still there – and brewing his own beer – in 1941.

Nowadays the ale sold is not brewed on the premises, but includes real ale from local breweries and also cider from local makers, to be enjoyed in the characterful interior with its many original features.

Still on display at the Chequers is this market sign, which indicated that the inn was allowed to sell 'intoxicating liquors' between 2.30 p.m. and 5 p.m. on Friday market day 'for the convenience of persons attending the public market'.

In the late nineteenth century, the Chequers was very much 'Biddle's House'.

The change in the façade over a period of 100 years can be seen by comparing the two photographs, the lower one of 1999.

A short distance from the town centre, westwards along Bargates, is the Radnorshire Arms, which started as the Fox Inn. This is one of the few establishments that can be reasonably dated, as when it was offered for sale by auction in 1840 it was said to be a 'Newly-erected FREEHOLD PUBLIC-HOUSE, called the FOX TAVERN, with the Stable, Garden, and enclosed Yard, with a private Driving Way,....' By 1856 Samuel Prosser was in charge, and about 1858 he changed the name to the Radnorshire Arms. The reason for the change has not so far been found – he certainly wasn't a native of Radnorshire, being born in Docklow, not far from Leominster. Apart from the public house, Samuel Prosser had a business as a carrier, with a regular trip to Eardisland, Pembridge and Kington starting from the Radnorshire Arms at 6 a.m. on a Tuesday. He also took his wagon to Worcester each Thursday, returning on the Saturday. Occasionally he went to Presteigne, so all in all he must have been busy, particularly as he also acted as a timber haulier. In the early 1880s his son James took over the licence, which he held for a few years, and in 1903, when John Bassett was the occupier, the owner of the property was Miss M.A. Prosser, of New Street, no doubt another member of the family.

This is an establishment that hasn't changed overmuch and in 2006 CAMRA described it as a 'workaday locals' two-bar pub...'

This view of England's Gate Inn, taken in the 1970s, differs little from that of today. A splendid timbered building, having its origins around the year 1600, it has been added to and altered over the years without spoiling its character. England's Gate was certainly an inn in the latter part of the eighteenth century, the landlord William Wood selling up in 1794. He was followed by John Grocott who, by 1806, had been succeeded by John Gillam (with several variant spellings!). In his time England's Gate was visited by the player Mr Moon, whose visit was reported in the *Hereford Journal* of 1 February 1815: 'The performances of the celebrated Mr Moon, closed on Wednesday at Englands Gate, when he received that applause which is certainly his due, and the room was so crowded on each night of exhibition, that several were obliged to depart without witnessing his entertaining performance'. Frustratingly, it was not stated what Moon's performances were about!

Gillam was there until at least the mid-1820s, and he was succeeded by James Roberts, in whose time the local Ledbury and Leominster Turnpike Trust started to hold its meetings at the inn. Roberts defaulted on his rent to the Hampton Court Estate and in consequence his post horses and furniture were disposed of in two sales, in 1834 and 1835. George Cox, his successor, was more successful, and leased the property until about 1849, when he was succeeded by Francis Green, who was here until the mid-1860s. Succeeded by Christopher Robinson, by 1870 it had been taken over by William Purchase, and various members of this family rented the inn until the early years of the twentieth century. In 1903 the inn was still owned by the Hampton Court Estate, but was subsequently sold. In the 1980s and 1990s England Gate was closed for a while but was restored and is now thriving.

WITH POSSESSION ON COMPLETION OF PURCHASE.

HEREFORDSHIRE.

PARISH OF WELLINGTON.

𝔓articulars of 𝔖ale

OF

A FREEHOLD PROPERTY

FORMERLY KNOWN AS

" THE BRIDGE INN "

ALSO A

VALUABLE ENCLOSURE OF PASTURE LAND

To be offered for SALE BY AUCTION by

APPERLEY & BROWN

AT THE

LAW SOCIETY'S ROOMS, EAST STREET, HEREFORD,

ON WEDNESDAY, 30th JUNE, 1926

~~AT 3 O'CLOCK~~ AT 2-30 P.M.

(unless previously disposed of),

Subject to " The General Conditions of 1925," incorporating the Common Form Conditions of the Herefordshire Law Society.

For further Particulars and Permission to View apply to

Messrs. OSBORNE, WARD, VASSALL, ABBOT & Co., Solicitors, Bristol ;

T. A. MATTHEWS, Solicitors, Hereford ; *or to*

THE AUCTIONEERS, BANK CHAMBERS, HEREFORD, at whose Offices Plans of the Properties may be inspected.

The Hereford Times Ltd., Printers.

Midway between Hereford and Leominster on the turn to Wellington village is a large group of buildings, pictured above in 1999 in a dilapidated state, but now restored. This was formerly the main inn between Hereford and Leominster, called the King's Arms, but generally known as the Bridge Inn. In 1772 this brick-built inn was advertised as being to let either as an inn or a private house. It continued as an inn, but with varying degrees of success. John Mellin, who seems to have taken over from E. Bethell in 1810, got into financial difficulties and as a result had his household goods sold by auction in December 1817. The inn was subsequently advertised as being to let, together with twenty-five statute acres. Mellin seems to have recovered from his troubles, as a person with this unusual name was licensee for a few years from 1823 onwards. In the 1830s and 1840s there was a succession of landlords, none seeming to stay for long. Thus in 1841, after only a few years at the Bridge Inn, Henry Clarke moved to the Maidenhead, Orleton, to be succeeded in Wellington by Thomas Preece of the Orange Tree, Hereford. Preece was replaced by James Pitt in 1846, but within less than two years Joseph Walters had taken over; he died in 1850 at the age of fifty-one. In the 1850s Frederick Bishop took over, and was licensee until at least 1871, breaking the run of bad luck. In 1882 a visit was made to the Bridge Inn by members of the renowned Woolhope Club, but only to leave their carriages while they 'walked on the raised path by the brook lane to Wellington church'. The present road to Wellington by the side of the Bridge Inn was not made until the early years of the twentieth century.

The Bridge Inn seems to have declined in the twentieth century, and had closed by the time it was offered for sale by auction on 30 June 1926, when it was bought by a local man for £160. The title page of the sale particulars is illustrated on the opposite page. The building has been somewhat restored but is again on the market.

The top photograph of the Red Lion, Monkland was taken before it was burnt down in 1910 and its replacement building, illustrated below in a recent photograph, is typical of that period. In the first part of the nineteenth century it was called the Travellers' Rest, the name being changed to the Red Lion before 1851. At the beginning of the twentieth century the landlord was Frank Webb, and the inn was owned by the brewers Lane Bros & Bastow of Ledbury. By 1909 Webb had been succeeded by William Price, who must have been here when the inn burnt down. Fortunately it was rebuilt by the owners and carried on serving the public. William Day Williams, licensee here in the 1920s and 1930s, took advantage of the roadside position and advertised teas and light refreshment. Like so many inns, it has had another name change, and is now called the Monkland Arms. It reopened in 2008 after being closed since the previous year.

The Mortimer's Cross Inn is slightly down-at-heel in this 1999 photograph, but has since been restored and refurbished and its facilities are now suitable for the twenty-first century. Near the site of the battle of Mortimer's Cross, it was built in the early eighteenth century. Towards the end of that century and until the turnpike trusts were abolished in the 1860s, it was where the Presteigne and Blue Mantle Hall Turnpike Trusts held their meetings. In 1780 Edward Bradford took over the inn, and members of his family were here until the late 1870s, not quite a century! In the 1850s and 1860s there was an annual ploughing match based at the inn, with a celebration afterwards. In 1867 it was reported that there was a dinner afterwards at the Mortimer's Cross Inn 'the house of one of the most respected and jolliest of men, Mr John Bradford...'. In 1890 it was the headquarters of the Shobdon Fishing Club and advertised, 'Good beds and every accommodation for travellers & anglers'. John Payne, the owner and proprietor around the turn of the twentieth century, called it a 'Hotel'. For much of the twentieth century there is little to record, but the prospects for the twenty-first century look much brighter.

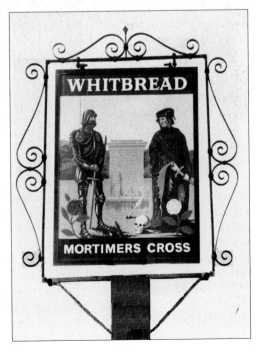

Anyone emulating the working man in this 1920s photograph of Wigmore would not last long! In the middle is the Castle Inn, burnt down in 1928, although the stables survived until 1966. The inn was built in 1721 and was the centre for village activities. In the early nineteenth century it was the place where meetings were held about the Wigmore Inclosure Act, and a plan under the proposed Act was left with Mr Crump, the landlord. In 1847 the Wigmore Female Friendly Society was started, based at the Castle Inn, a club later referred to as the Wigmore Sick Society – no Welfare State then. At this period the landlord, John Phippen, also acted as postmaster. He left in 1863, and Charles Harrison, his successor, was in trouble with the magistrates in 1867 for allowing drunkenness on the premises. Thomas Evans, here by 1885 and still here in 1909, advertised 'Comfortable accommodation for travellers. Good stabling. Headquarters C.T.C.' The inn belonged to the Harley estate of Brampton Bryan, a loss to the estate when it was burnt down.

The Olde Oak, one of the two surviving inns in Wigmore, began as a beerhouse in the 1860s, and was run by William Burgoyne, a stonemason. He was succeeded by his widow Elizabeth, who was still there in 1909. A full licence was finally granted as recently as 1961.

The Compasses Inn in Wigmore became licensed some time after 1828, and was in existence by 1841 when John Thomas was the licensee. Two years later Benjamin Pollard had difficulty in obtaining a licence, and when he did so he advertised in the *Hereford Times* his thanks 'to those Gentlemen and others who kindly interfered for him...' assuring them that 'it will at all times be his anxious study to make his house deserving of their patronage and support'. In 1844 a Lodge of the Independent Order of Odd Fellows, Manchester Unity, was set up here.

One notable incident took place here in April 1866. This was an inquest held before H. Moore, coroner for the division, enquiring into the death of twelve-year-old Arthur Thomson, son of Harriet Thomson, the landlady, who had succeeded her late husband in the licence. The lad had had his left arm broken on two occasions, the last occasion being about five months previously. Prior to his death he had played truant from Lucton School for several days, for which he was caned by the master and flogged by his brother. After his death the rumour spread that he had been flogged too severely by the master, and feelings ran high, but other pupils proved that this was not the case. The report in the newspaper concluded, 'He was taken ill on Saturday and died on Tuesday, and the medical gentleman gave it as his opinion that death was caused from gastric fever and congestion of the lungs, accelerated by injuries to the arm; but how the injuries were received remain a mystery. The Jury returned a verdict accordingly, and did not attribute blame to anyone'.

Business may have been slow at the Compasses, and many of the licensees had other jobs. Stephen Staley, here in the late 1850s was a plumber, painter and glazier; in the 1870s John Vale was also a carpenter and joiner; while Joshua Gillam, here by 1890 until his death in 1898, was a baker. Gilliam's successor, Thomas Simonson, was a very busy man, as he was also a baker, grocer, and draper, tea and provision dealer. While Simonson was the licensee, the inn was owned by the Ludlow Brewery Company. Archie Miles was here in the 1920s, and in the 1930s, probably during his time, the Compasses was extended. His successor, Miss Mabel Price, dignified the Compasses by calling it a hotel, rather than an inn, which it is still called today.

This discreet sign for the Sun Inn, in Rosemary Lane, Leintwardine, is the only indication of a truly rare survival of a simple beer-house. So rare, in fact, that it is on CAMRA's National Inventory of pub interiors, with no bar as such and only a simple parlour with benches and scrubbed tables. Being a beer-house, it has little in the way of recorded history. It was started by William Jones in the early 1860s, probably to supplement his income as a tailor, and after his death in 1878 his widow Sarah kept it for a while, until she retired. James Savager succeeded her, and was here by 1881. He stayed for a few years, but moved on to the Cooper's Arms, Leintwardine, being succeeded at the Sun Inn by John Lippett; the names of both James and John Lippett occur between 1890 and 1909. In 1903 the beer-house was run by James Lippett and owned by Ann Allum, of The Compasses, Ludlow. In the 1920s and 1930s Charles Lane was the licensee, and he was succeeded by his widow Mary. It is still in the same family, with loyal locals helping with the day-to-day running of the pub.

The Lion Hotel, Leintwardine, is of some considerable age as a licensed house, and in 1811 it was stated, 'The Red Lion Inn, situated near the bridge, affords neat and good accommodation for travellers'. William Evans probably took over the licence in 1812, after the death of the former licensee, and he was here until 1838. Such was the esteem in which he was held, that when he died in 1850 the notice of his death in the *Hereford Journal* stated that he was 'many years the highly respected landlord of the Lion Inn'. From the middle of the nineteenth century the inn was more usually referred to as the Lion Hotel. In 1890 Charles Samuel Hall, the then licensee, advertised that the Lion Hotel offered 'comfortable accommodation for travellers and visitors, good posting house'. Alterations in the 1950s changed the emphasis from hotel to inn and restaurant, benefiting from its attractive location by the bridge and river.

3

BROMYARD AND NEARBY

A modern photograph of the Queen's Arms, High Street, Bromyard. The entry at the side has been known as the Leopard entry since the eighteenth century.

While the King's Arms in Bromyard – seen above in a photograph of 1999 – has largely been re-fronted, it is of considerable age.

The front block dates from the early seventeenth century, and the south-eastern part is about 100 years older. It also boasts the largest chimney in the area. Certainly it was an inn in the early eighteenth century, if not before. At that time, and later, the High Street in front of the King's Arms was used as a beast market, where cattle were sold on market day, and no doubt the inn benefited from this. The inn was sold for £1,000 in 1819, while in 1890 it was sold for £1,200, not a great increase. It was sold by auction in 1907, and the details shown opposite give a good description of the property. In 1920 it was sold yet again, when it fetched £2,400.

Bromyard did not get electric light until 1923, and at that time a wireless was installed at the King's Arms for the benefit of customers. At this time the large yard to the rear was used as a market for poultry and produce, and during the last war this housed elephants from a circus that was staying in the vicinity for the duration of the war. The market continued both during and after the war, but in 1969 there were objections from the local tradespeople, and the market closed.

PARTICULARS.

———◆———

The well-frequented, old-established, FREE and FULL-LICENSED FREEHOLD

COMMERCIAL AND MARKET HOUSE

KNOWN AS

"The King's Arms,"

TO BE SOLD BY AUCTION BY

BENTLEY, HOBBS & MYTTON

At the King's Arms, Bromyard,

On Thursday, 31st October, 1907,

At **2-30** for **3-30** p.m. punctually, by direction of the Executors of the late Mrs. ANN PARTRIDGE.

———

The Accommodation comprises—ON THE GROUND FLOOR: Capital large Bar, Dining Room, 22ft. by 12ft. 4in., Commercial Room 17ft. by 11ft., Back Parlour, Tap Room with Fire Place, Kitchen with Range and Sink, Pantry with Store Room over and Coal House.

ON THE FIRST FLOOR: Large Front Dining Room with bay window, 25ft. by 16ft. 8in., and 4 Bedrooms.

ON THE SECOND FLOOR: 6 Bedrooms.

IN THE BASEMENT: Large Wine and Beer Cellars.

THE SPACIOUS YARD has two approaches, from Cruxwell Street and the New Road, and comprises BREWHOUSE with Two Furnaces and large Soft-water Tank, WASHING HOUSE with Furnace and Sink, extensive range of STABLING, 2 LOOSE BOXES with SADDLE ROOM and Loft over, Lean to Shed, Pigstye and Offices, Pump and good Supply of Water.

There is a LARGE KITCHEN GARDEN planted with Apple, Pear and Plum Trees, Poultry House with wire run, Pigstye and Offices.

THE PROPERTY is situate in a good position in the centre of the MARKET TOWN of BROMYARD, and is well worthy the attention of BREWERS, LICENSED VICTUALLERS and CAPITALISTS, a most LUCRATIVE BUSINESS having been carried on by the late Mr. and Mrs. Partridge for nearly FIFTY YEARS, and is now sold owing to their decease.

THE BUSINESS is being carried on by the Executors of the late Mrs. Partridge. POSSESSION WILL BE GIVEN ON COMPLETION OF THE PURCHASE.

The Purchaser will be required to take to all Trade and other Fixtures and Fittings, Stock-in-Trade, proportion of the Licenses, Assessments and other Payments at a valuation to be made in the usual way.

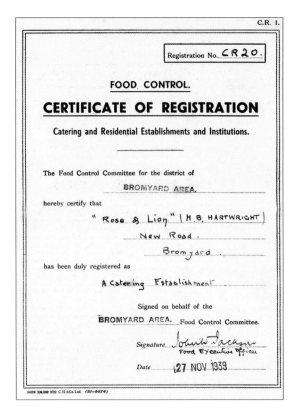

C.R. 1.

Registration No. CR 20.

FOOD CONTROL.

CERTIFICATE OF REGISTRATION

Catering and Residential Establishments and Institutions.

The Food Control Committee for the district of

BROMYARD AREA.

hereby certify that

" Rose & Lion " (H.B. HARTWRIGHT)

New Road.

Bromyard.

has been duly registered as

A Catering Establishment

Signed on behalf of the

BROMYARD AREA. Food Control Committee.

Signature John W. Jackson
Food Executive Officer

Date 27 NOV 1939

34098 300,000 3/39 C.H.&Co.Ltd. (51–4474)

The Rose and Lion, in New Road, is little changed from this photograph of the 1960s. It began as a beer-house around 1835, under the 1830 Act, although it subsequently obtained a full licence. In 1918 the then owner, a Mr Turbill, sold the pub at auction for £625. The purchaser was a local builder, who sold it on to a brewery in Worcester, who put George Royall in as tenant at an annual rent of £20. At this time the pub had a market licence, allowing it to remain open all day on a Thursday. During Royall's tenancy the custom of having an annual outing for regulars began, which continued when his son-in-law, Henry Ronald Hartwright, took over in 1932. At the outbreak of the Second World War, the Rose and Lion became registered as a catering establishment, the official certificate being illustrated here. Mr Hartwright died in 1965 and his widow carried on until her death in 1975.

The Rose and Lion, known simply as the Rosie, is now one of the two tied houses of the Wye Valley Brewery, and is an unspoilt traditional pub. Rent for the garden is paid in parsnips grown in the garden!

Almost directly opposite the bottom of New Road is the Queen's Arms, seen below in a photograph of 1999. This began as a private house, but became a public house called the Leopard around 1770. The parish registers record the burial, on 22 January 1792, of Thomas Elmore, 'a poor boy burnt to death at a Public House, called the Leopard, in this town, pauper'. For some years around 1800 the building was used as a bakery, but eventually reverted to licensed premises. There was a name change to the Wellington's Arms about the year 1820, then about ten years later to the Grey's Arms, or the Earl Grey. In 1833 the then licensee attempted to close the entry at the side of the Grey's Arms, which caused local disquiet, and it remained open. The final name change, to the Queen's Arms, had taken place by 1839, no doubt to celebrate the young Queen Victoria. However, old names linger on and in the early part of the twentieth century the entry at the side was still called the Leopard entry by old Bromyardians.

BROMYARD.

TO BE SOLD BY AUCTION, BY

BENTLEY, HOBBS & MYTTON

At The Queens Arms, Bromyard,

On TUESDAY, 5th JULY, 1921,

AT 3 P.M.

THE WELL-FREQUENTED OLD-ESTABLISHED FULLY-LICENSED FREEHOLD COMMERCIAL INN AND MARKET HOUSE,

Known as

"The Queen's Arms,"

With extensive Stabling, Yard and Offices, situate in High Street, in the centre of the Market Town of Bromyard and extending to Rowberry Street, within a few minutes' walk of the Railway Station and Cattle Market, at present let to Messrs. IND, COOPE AND COMPANY LIMITED, on lease expiring 29th September, 1921.

The Accommodation comprises, on the Ground Floor :—Entrance Passage; Front Bar with Bay Window 21ft. x 12ft. 9in., with Fireplace and Cupboard enclosed Folding Doors; Smoke Room with Bay Window 21ft. x 7ft. 9in. with Fireplace; Back Passage with Wine Cellar; Tap Room 14ft. 9in. x 9ft. 3in. with oven grate; Sitting Room 14ft. 6in. x 10ft. 10in. with two Cupboards enclosed Folding Doors and Shelves over and Fireplace; Old Bar with two Cupboards enclosed Folding Doors; Larder with Shelves; Kitchen with Range, having Sink with Tap of Water over, Double Cupboard enclosed Folding Doors and Plate Shelves; Wash House and W.C.; Large Store Room about 17ft. 5in. x 17ft. 5in.

On the 1st Floor.—Club Room 29ft. 2in. x 19ft. 4in., having one side panelled with old oak with handsomely carved frieze and two antique firegrates; Anti Room adjoining; Two Back Bedrooms with Fireplaces; and Box Room.

On the 2nd Floor :—Two Front Bedrooms with several pieces of Old Oak panelling and Small Cupboard; and two small Back Bedrooms.

The SPACIOUS YARD has two approaches from High Street and Rowberry Street and comprises Lean-to Store Shed; Stable to tie Eight Horses with Loft over; two-stall Stable with Loft over; Stable to tie 14 Horses with Loft over; and usual appurtenances.

THIS PROPERTY is situate in a good position in the centre of the Market Town of Bromyard, and is well worthy of the attention of Brewers, Licensed Victuallers and Capitalists, having a frontage to High Street of about 30ft. 6in. with Driving Way to Back Yard, and extending to Rowberry Street at which there is a Frontage of about 33ft. 6in.

Town Water and Gas laid on.

The Lessees claim certain fixtures—a list will be supplied at the sale.

In 1906 the landlord, Edward King, became bankrupt, and the Queen's Arms was sold. It was sold again in 1921, the sale particulars illustrated above giving a good description of what was the pub was like at that time.

This is yet another half-timbered building but again with a more recent front, it was built in the late sixteenth century and has a contemporary staircase with round newel post and steps.

The Bay Horse was formed by the amalgamation of two adjacent properties, as this 1999 photograph clearly shows. On the left-hand side was the Black Swan, while on the right-hand side was the Castle Inn, which absorbed the Black Swan. Somewhere about the year 1802 William Devereux took over the inn, and it was probably about this time that the name was changed. It was held by four members of the family, who were much interested in horses and racing. George Devereux, who died in 1878, had a stud of thoroughbred horses, which were kept in the yard to the rear of the inn. This area later became a slaughterhouse which, in the 1930s, was much used by the country people who slaughtered and sold their own meat.

In the 1980s the Bay Horse was refurbished, losing much of its character in the process. It was then closed and neglected for some years, until a new owner carefully restored the interior, undoing the previous work. The original entry was from the large yard at the rear, evidence of its former use as a coaching inn.

This sketch of the Hop Pole in the Square at Bromyard (above) shows it partly obscured by the old market hall which was removed in 1844, leaving the inn in full view. There was an earlier inn in the square called the Nag's Head, taken over by Edward Williams in 1765, and he was still there in 1767. Late in 1768 Edward Williams was at the Hop Pole, suggesting that he was the first licensee. Behind the inn, on the opposite side of Rowberry Street, there was extensive stabling for horses. Williams was a busy man, being also a maltster. He died in 1794, having been the landlord for at least twenty-six years.

The Hop Pole was involved in posting, and in 1867 was advertised as a 'Family, Commercial, and Posting house, and Inland Revenue office'. At this time it was run by D.W. Cottrell, whose name appears on this bill of 1877. Posting was still offered at the beginning of the twentieth century, when it was ended by the advent of cars.

In 2002 the Hop Pole, including the stabling and car park across the road, was sold by auction for £180,000. Since then the stables have been converted to houses, no doubt much more profitable!

For the Prefervation of the GAME.

AT two feveral Meetings held at the Falcon, in Bromyard, the 31ft of January, and the 7th of February, 1785, it was agreed, that any perfon who will give information of any poachers, or unqualified perfons, who fhall kill or deftroy any hare, pheafant, or partridge, to convict him thereof, fhall receive TWO GUINEAS from the Treafurer of this Society, over and above the reward intitled unto by Act of Parliament; and particularly for every hare killed by tracing in a fnow, fhall receive the fum of FOUR GUINEAS, befides the reward intitled unto by Act of Parliament, by applying at the Whitehoufe, in Suckley, to

THO. FREEMAN, jun.
Solicitor and Treafurer to the faid Society.

JOHN BARNEBY,
THOMAS TOMKYNS,
RICHARD CHAMBERS,   } Efquires.
JOHN FREEMAN,
THO. FREEMAN,
JOS. SEVERNE,
RICHARD JONES.
WILLIAM LAWRENCE.

N. B. Meetings held firft Monday in every month, at the Falcon, to receive fubfcriptions and information.

In this early-twentieth century photograph of Bromyard (opposite above), looking from the High Street to Broad Street, the timberwork of the Falcon is covered with plaster, as it had been for many years. In 1883 the local newspaper reported that the plaster was beginning to fall off, and that it was hoped it would be restored to a timber frontage again. However, this did not happen until 1933, when the removal of the plaster revealed how the roof had been raised to give another storey. The Bishop of Hereford was lord of the manor, and the manorial court met here as the most important inn in the town. At one court in the eighteenth century a pain or penalty of £1 19s was laid upon all victuallers and innholders who did not sell a full measure, a ruling we can applaud! The trustees of the Bromyard Turnpike Trust met in the Falcon, and the tolls were let by auction here, not always successfully. Meetings of the trustees and other matters of public interest were usually advertised in the *Hereford Journal*. There was a local society for the preservation of game, which offered rewards for information leading to the successful conviction of poachers, a sample advert of 1785 being illustrated here (opposite).

The Bromyard Assembly also met regularly in the winter months in the large assembly room. Balls to celebrate national events were held here. Thus, when Napoleon was exiled to Elba in 1814, a very successful ball was held – more successful than Napoleon's captivity, for he subsequently escaped, only to be finally defeated at the battle of Waterloo in 1815. In modern publicity the ballroom is one of the facilities advertised as well as the ten en-suite bedrooms.

At the rear of the Falcon and fronting onto Pump Street is a long building which was used as a cinema. First called the Rio, and then the Plaza, it opened in August 1948, and closed in 1963. Unused for many years, it has recently been refurbished in medieval style as further accommodation, and is now called Falcon Mews.

The early nineteenth-century front of the Crown and Sceptre in Sherford Street, with cast iron columns to the portico, conceals a timber-framed building. Beneath is a cellar through which the Bibble Brook flows (or rather, trickles!). The earlier name for the inn was the Queen's Head, but this changed to the Crown and Sceptre in the 1820s, possibly at the time the front was rebuilt. In the 1830s the stables to the rear were used by carriers, with regular wagons to Hereford and Worcester.

Sherford Street leads to Church Street where there was the Railway Inn, closed in the 1970s, but still with a sign indicating its former use. This was the favourite watering hole of the church bell ringers, seen here in the bar in a jovial mood. They were most upset when the pub closed!

Walter Williams, landlord of the Burley Gate Inn, is probably the gentleman holding the tray in this carefully posed photograph of around 1905 outside the inn. This inn has several other names – probably the Plough Inn mentioned in 1802 and the Jolly Crispin in 1815, both at Burley Gate. Certainly it was called the Mason's Arms when James Hodges ran it in the 1830s and 1840s, not too surprising since he was also a stone mason. In the 1890s the landlord was Thomas Ovens, a retired policeman, and his successor was Walter Williams, another retired policeman, who died in 1911. His widow married again, for the third time, to an Isaac Davies who travelled the area with shire horses and used the Burley Gate Inn as a base. After the death of Mrs Davies, her husband ran the pub until his death just before the Second World War, when it was then sold to a brewery. It closed about 1990, and is now a private house, with another house built in its grounds.

In the early 1920s Florence (Florrie) Badham worked at the Burley Gate Inn, as a barmaid, and kept a record of her wages, one page of which is reproduced here. She was paid £1 13s 4d a month – no minimum wage then!

The Live and Let Live is one of the oldest buildings on the part of Bringsty Common that lies in Bromyard parish, and dates from around 1700. Its use as licensed premises seems to date from the middle of the nineteenth century when the tenant, Samuel Harris, was running a cider-house. By 1859 he was also keeping a shop, and so subsequently did his widow and son. At the beginning of the next century Edmund Morgan ran what was still a beer and cider-house, and this photograph of around 1910 (opposite above) is probably of him and his family outside the inn. He died in 1918 at the age of seventy-five. Subsequently the thatch was replaced by tiles, although the distinctive 'eyebrow' window at the front gave the clue that it had formerly been thatched.

From 1955 until 1991 the pub was run by Don and Mavis Griffiths, with Don also working as the postman for the Common. In that year he retired, the brewery having a rule that a tenant had to retire at the age of sixty-five, and the pub was then sold. In 1996, after the owner had tried unsuccessfully to sell the pub as a business, an application was made to turn it into a private residence, but this was turned down (opposite below, the pub in 1996). Eventually, after four planning enquiries, in 2002 the pub was sold, although in the interim the building had deteriorated to such an extent that the new owner had to move into a static home. An idea of the state of the building can be gained from the photograph taken in 2002 (above). But happily the building has now been completely restored and the thatch replaced. It reopened for business in November 2007. The Live and Let Live lives yet again!

Joseph Wood, landlord of the King's Head at Docklow (above, in 2000) in the middle of the nineteenth century, was also a blacksmith and implement maker, and would have benefited from the position by the side of the turnpike road from Bromyard to Leominster, and on to Aberystwyth. In recent years the licence has changed hands a couple of times and the inn has been smartened up; the restaurant also sometimes doubles as a meeting room. The inn has also featured favourably in an article that appeared in the *Independent* in 2006, by a leader writer living locally.

In the middle of the nineteenth century Thomas Potter, the licensee of the Plough at Stoke Lacy (above, in 1999), was described as a blacksmith and victualler, clerk and sexton, so must have been very busy. In 1938 William Symonds moved the family cider-making business to a site behind the Plough, and he was also the licensee. In the early 1980s the pub was bought by Greenall Whitley, which also bought the cider-making business. It is now a flourishing local pub with an emphasis on food. As for the cider business, since 2002 the premises have been the home of the Wye Valley Brewery, moving here from outgrown premises at the Barrels Inn in St Owen's Street, Hereford.

4

LEDBURY AND EAST HEREFORDSHIRE

This trap must be delivering milk, not ale, to the Brewery Inn, Bye
Street, Ledbury in the early years of the twentieth century.

Because of the rising ground behind the building, the steps up to the Horse Shoe Inn in the Homend, Ledbury, are necessary. However, in the days when cattle were sold in the street outside the inn, the auctioneer took advantage, and stood on top of the steps to conduct his business. As a consequence the inn did much trade on market days. William Pain, licensee by 1790, was also a carpenter, so must have been busy. The inn was in the hands of various members of the Pain family until at least the mid-1830s. While this seventeenth-century building has undergone many alterations over its long history, many original features would be recognised by these early licensees.

This view up Church Street is one of the most iconic images of Ledbury. Always prominent in the view is the Prince of Wales, a building dating from the late sixteenth century, with its main entrance in Church Lane and a small rear entrance in Church Street. As a pub it had its origins in the 1830s when Richard Tyler, a shoe, patten and clog maker supplemented his income by running a beer-house. Subsequently gaining a full licence, the licensee in the 1930s was still brewing his own beer. Now the emphasis is on real ales and good food.

In the early nineteenth century the Seven Stars (top, in early 2001) was owned and run by William Barrett, who was well enough off to ride to hounds in scarlet. In his time there were also old oak seats fitted on either side of the entrance. The Seven Stars was not as fortunate as the Horse Shoe up the road, as on market day the pigs were penned opposite the Seven Stars! A later licensee, Harry Tarbath, who died in 1932, in his younger days used to drive the horse mail coach between Bromyard and Worcester, and also a four-in-hand stage coach between Ledbury and Gloucester until the building of the Ledbury/Gloucester railway line over the line of the old canal in the early 1880s.

The Seven Stars, one of the historic inns of Ledbury, was devastated by a fire in July 2001, (above) but has since risen, phoenix-like, from the ashes after a careful restoration and it is difficult to tell that anything had happened.

The problem with timbered buildings is water penetration, and such buildings were often rendered to make them weather tight. The photograph of the Talbot (right), treated in this way, was taken in the 1880s when C.C. Wetson was landlord, but within a few years this had been stripped off, the building renovated, and the windows altered (below). The inn was called, almost inevitably, Ye Olde Talbot. A framed list of licensees appears inside the pub, reaching back into the eighteenth century. Among them were Leslie and Gwendoline Wrist, here from 1948 until 1966. In their time they were host to, among others, Boris Karloff, famous as Frankenstein's monster. They also had a Labrador dog that was trained to ring a handbell in its teeth – surely a most unusual way to call time!

The street scene on the opposite page taken in the early years of the twentieth century, looking up New Street towards the Upper Cross, reflects a quieter way of life, with only the early car with registration plate CJ 32

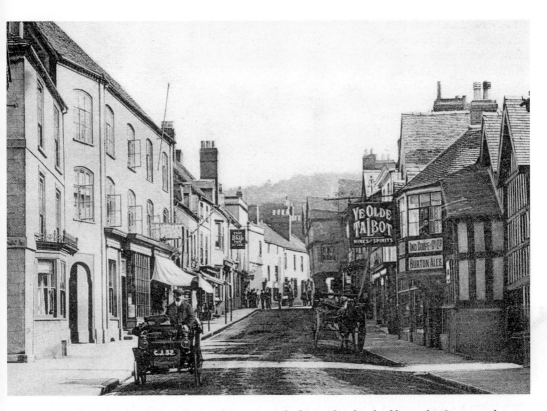

as a foretaste of what was to come. This car is parked outside what had been the Crown and Sceptre, a short-lived inn that closed around 1880. The sign for the Bell Inn can be seen, an

inn that closed about 1930 and is now almost unrecognisable after drastic alteration. The Talbot, however, is still there and flourishing. Inside is a glorious panelled room (right), the original fireplace of which is flanked by tapering Ionic pilasters and has a decorated overmantel. Opposite the fireplace is a central Ionic pilaster, which bears the initials and date A.N. 1596, no doubt the date when the panelling was installed. In the next century the room entered the pages of history, for it is said that it was the scene of a clash between Prince Rupert's men and a few of Cromwell's soldiers who had been cut off after the Battle of Ledbury.

The omnibus waits outside the Feathers Hotel, *c.* 1890.

The Feathers stripped of its plaster coat, *c.* 1910,

The following is a reproduction of a billhead:

FEATHERS HOTEL LIVERY STABLES AND GARAGE,
Ledbury, Nov 191

DR. TO T. HOWELL,

OPEN and CLOSED MOTORS FOR HIRE.
PETROL. . . .
REPAIRS. . . .
ACCESSORIES . .

POSTING IN ALL ITS BRANCHES.
Good Stabling.   Lock-up Coach House.
OMNIBUS MEETS ALL TRAINS.

Customers' Cars are only driven by own staff at Customers' own risk and responsibility.

Telegraphic Address: "Feathers, Ledbury."   Telephone: P.O. 6.

1914
Aug 5   Hire of 4 doz Table Forks   £2 5 3
4 doz Dessert Forks, 4 dz Dessert Spoons
4 doz Tea Spoons &c   8/=

21/11/14   Paid Thos Howell with thanks

Lady Biddulph   charged

The Feathers Hotel is another splendid timbered building, made up of two houses. That on the left was built around 1560-70 and the right-hand part built in the early seventeenth century. Like the Talbot, it was all formerly rendered and its drab appearance is clear in the photograph of around 1890 (opposite above), enlivened by the horse-drawn omnibus that met all trains at Ledbury station and took guests to the Feathers. With the removal of the render, the appearance was greatly improved, as demonstrated in this photograph of around 1910 (opposite below), when the car age had come and it was found necessary to advertise garage accommodation.

The original name of the hotel was the Plume of Feathers, inevitably shortened to the Feathers. In the early eighteenth century it belonged to the Biddulph estate, and in 1719 was rented out, furnished, for an annual rent of £9! In the late eighteenth century the landlord was Luke Morris, who, in 1773, took over the King's Arms – an inn directly over the road from the Plume of Feathers – which he promptly closed down. In 1797 Morris was succeeded by Giles Taylor, and members of his family were there until at least the middle 1830s. The Plume of Feathers was also the Post Office and Excise Office, and as such it remained until at least the middle of the nineteenth century. It was also a coaching inn and posting house and the six post boys who were kept here, were splendidly dressed in breeches, yellow jackets and white top hats, with top boots, spurs and whips. As the leading inn in the town, the Royal Mail coach from London stopped here, before carrying on to Hereford, where it made a connection to Aberystwyth. Up to 1885 the Gloucester mail coach started from the Feathers at 8 a.m. and called at Dymock and Newent on its way to Gloucester, returning to Ledbury at 6.00 p.m.

There was also a large Assembly Room, where the Ledbury Assembly was held. In the winter of 1836 John Biddulph was shocked to witness waltzing at a ball in the Feathers Assembly Room, the more so since his daughters participated in it. How times have changed! Another change from the beginning of the twentieth century was the addition of a garage to the livery stables, proudly proclaimed on the billhead above, dating from 1914.

The Feathers has benefitted from being in the same ownership since 1970, and modern facilities include a leisure centre and conference rooms. The photograph above was taken in 2001 and shows little change from that of 1910.

78. The Southend, Ledbury

THE ROYAL OAK

1420 – REAR PART OF BUILDING CONSTRUCTED. USED AS A CIDER HOUSE.

1520 – FRONT PART BUILT AS SEPARATE HOUSE. USED AS ACCOMMODATION.

1645 – THE BUILDINGS JOINED TOGETHER AND USED AS A COACHING INN.

1856 – BRICK FACADE ADDED TO THE FRONT AND ALL EXPOSED INTERIOR BEAMS COVERED UP.

1998 – RESTORED AS NEAR AS POSSIBLE TO ITS ORIGINAL STATE.

Above: This carefully posed photograph of the Royal Oak in Southend was published as a postcard around 1910 by Luke Tilley & Son, Ledbury. Hidden behind the brick façade, now colour-washed, is a late sixteenth-century timber-framed building, and a room inside is panelled. A plaque on the outside of the building suggests that it has been used as an inn since 1645 (left) On 14 September 1790 a licence was granted to Richard Amey of the Royal 'Oake', victualler, but it is not known if it was the first that he had been granted. Succeeded by his widow Mary, she was here until at least 1841. A Friendly Society was founded here in 1816, the feast day of which was to be held on the morrow after Christmas – Boxing Day – 'the same to be continued for ever'. Regrettably this had lapsed by the middle of the century!

Behind the Royal Oak is what was called the Royal Hall, the entrance to which was underneath the canopy, which is prominent in the photograph. In 1902 it was reported that it was licensed for stage plays and it was claimed that the hall could seat about 500 people. In 1934 the Hall was bought by Eastnor Lodge of Freemasons, but in recent years it again came into the same ownership as the Royal Oak.

This dramatic photograph of an accident outside the Chase Inn, Bishop's Frome, was taken in the early 1950s, when a lorry coming down the hill from the Bromyard direction failed to negotiate the bend. The Chase was built around 1860, on a site that overlooks the village green. For many years there was a butcher's shop run with the inn, and in 1926 the largest complex of hop kilns in the country were built behind it.

Round the corner from the Chase Inn is the Green Dragon, whose jolly sign, painted in 1980 by a local artist, sports this impression of an inebriated dragon! The building dates from the seventeenth century, and has been an inn since at least the late eighteenth century. Philip Dutson was landlord by 1812 and members of his family held the licence until about 1970, a truly remarkable record. Inside, the inn is still unspoilt, a testimony to the care with which the Dutson family looked after it, with low beams, flagstone floors, and a large inglenook in the main bar.

The Seven Stars at Stifford's Bridge was known by that name for at least 200 years, but in 2002 it was renamed the Prancing Pony, and a few months later the bay window at the front was replaced by the present conservatory.

Over the road from the Prancing Pony is the much more dignified Red Lion, a building of seventeenth century origins but with later additions and alterations. It too was an inn in the eighteenth century, a testimony to the amount of passing trade which supported two inns in such close proximity well away from any main centre of population.

Above and right: One of the landmarks on the Hereford – Worcester road is the crossroads at Newtown, where, not too surprisingly, there is an inn. Formerly called the New Inn, in the middle of the twentieth century it became the Newtown Inn. It has a splendid three-dimensional sign, featuring a finger post showing the various destinations from the crossroads, now slightly dilapidated.

It must be the cyclists who are admiring the early car outside the then Foley Arms, Tarrington, in the 1920s. This splendid red-brick building dates from the eighteenth century, when it was known as the New Inn, the name being changed early in the nineteenth century to the Foley Arms as it belonged to the Stoke Edith estate, owned by the Foley family. Accommodation and food was also offered at the Foley Arms and on 11 August 1787 the Hon. John Byng noted in his diary, 'To recruit my spirits I stop'd at the village of Tarrington and eat bread and cheese; and drank brandy and water, which forced me along with more alacrity'. A later guest was one Levi Parker, a pig dealer from Ledbury, who stayed there on the night of 28 February 1832. He must have slept in the attic, for a newspaper report says that, walking in his sleep, he fell more than 30ft into a garden plot in front of the inn. Remarkably uninjured, he attended market in Hereford the following day!

In 1919 the Foley Arms was one of several properties from the Foley Estate that were offered for auction. In recent years the inn has had a varied history, with one episode when it was called the Glass Pig, an undignified name for a very dignified building. Now, however, it is called the Tarrington Arms, and offers a welcome stopping place on the road from Hereford to Ledbury.

Right: The inn sign in the 1960s.

At Hagley, usually incorrectly stated to be in Bartestree, is the New Inn, a former private residence built in 1880 for a member of the Godwin family of tile makers. The cellars are lined with a wide variety of tiles, evidently left over from various types that the factory made, producing an amazing effect. It became an inn at the end of the nineteenth century when the area was much less populated, and has benefited from the post-war expansion as a dormitory area for Hereford.

This photographic postcard of the Crown and Anchor at Lugwardine dates from around 1900. The building dates from the seventeenth century, with eighteenth century and later additions, and is immediately recognisable today. In the nineteenth century it was one of the inns that belonged to Watkins' Imperial Brewery, and was sold with the rest of the brewery in 1898. It is the place where the Lugg Commoners meet, and benefits from the increased local population and its proximity to the Tupsley area of Hereford.

5

ROSS AND SOUTH-WEST HEREFORDSHIRE

After the lunar landing in 1969, the name of the New Inn, Broad
Street, Ross, was changed to the Eagle in commemoration.

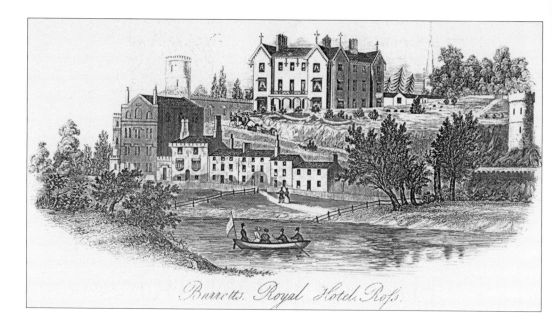

Barretts. Royal Hotel Ross.

Above: This mid-nineteenth century engraving of Barrett's Royal Hotel emphasises its prominent position overlooking the River Wye. The foundation stone was laid in 1837 with Masonic ceremony, James Barrett being a member of the local Vitruvian Lodge of Freemasons. The newspaper report calls it the Prospect Hotel, a reference to the fact that it was built on part of the area known as the Prospect, which had been bequeathed to the citizens of Ross in perpetuity by John Kyrle when he died in 1724. Barrett had purchased the old Pounds Inn, adjacent to the churchyard, which he had demolished. When the foundations of his new hotel were laid, an underground dungeon was found which had formed part of a former bishop's palace.

ROSS TO CHEPSTOW,
ALONG THE VALLEY OF THE WYE.

A SUPERIOR FOUR-HORSE COACH,
"THE TOURIST,"

in connection with the Great Western Railway, leaves the Station and Barrett's Royal Hotel, Ross, on the arrival of the first trains from Cheltenham, Gloucester, Hereford and Shrewsbury, for Monmouth, Tintern Abbey and Chepstow, reaching the latter place in time for trains to all parts of South Wales. Returning from the Railway Station and principal Hotels, Chepstow, after the arrival of the express trains from London and South Wales, passing through St. Arvans, Tintern Abbey, Landogo and Redbrook, arriving at the King's Head Hotel, Monmouth, at 4.30 P.M., and Barrett's Royal Hotel, and the Railway Station, Ross, in time for trains to the North and West of England and mail to London.

Passengers are allowed time to view the ruins of Tintern Abbey going and returning.

JAMES BARRETT, JOHN WEBB, WILLIAM SNOWDEN,
June, 1856. *Proprietors.*

old Pounds Inn, adjacent to the churchyard, which he had demolished. When the foundations of his new hotel were laid, an underground dungeon was found which had formed part of a former bishop's palace.

Just visible in the print, on the slope in front of the hotel, is a coach and horses. Naturally such a prominent place was a starting and finishing point for coaches, such as the one in this advertisement of 1856. In 1858 there was another coach (daily, except for Sundays) from the Royal Hotel to Monmouth, appropriately called 'the Tourist'. The Royal Hotel was described as a 'favourite starting point of summer parties who make the celebrated tour of the river Wye'. Perhaps the tourists in the boat visible in the engraving came from the Royal Hotel!

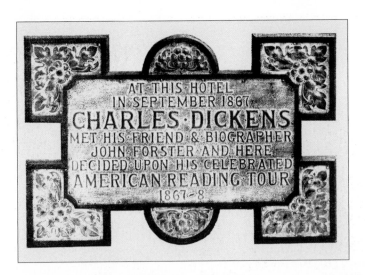

Above: Naturally such a prominent hotel, described in publicity material in the twentieth century as 'the best Hotel in the Wye Valley', has had many important and noteworthy visitors, many of whom came to enjoy the Wye tour. Every effort was made to accommodate this wish, and in June 1841 an advertisement appeared in the *Hereford Journal*, wanting to hire three or four pleasure boats for the benefit of visitors to the Royal Hotel. Not all visitors were for the tour, however, nor could all visitors be marked with a plaque such as this, erected to commemorate the visit of Charles Dickens in 1867.

Below: On 3 September 1891 a Royal party visited the hotel, and signed their names in the visitors' book. The party, which included Princess Mary of Teck (later Queen Mary), her parents the Duke and Duchess of Teck, and brother Prince Alexander George of Teck, took a boat from Ross to Symond's Yat, having luncheon at Goodrich Court on the way.

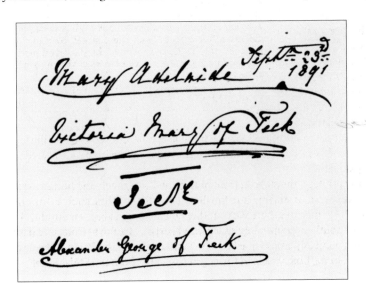

Above left: The mock medieval walls of Ross, built in the 1830s, look down on a small square. Facing the walls is the Man of Ross inn, named after Ross's greatest benefactor, John Kyrle. There have been a few changes to this elevation since this mid-twentieth century photograph was taken, and the name is not now nearly so prominent.

Above right: The single-storey extension with the high Dutch-style gable houses the bar, while the main building, which dates from the seventeenth century, has been much altered over the years. It was only in the 1840s that this inn was opened, so the name must have been intended to capitalize on John Kyrle's fame. He died in 1724 and eight years later his good works were eulogised in a poem by Alexander Pope, which gave him the soubriquet 'The Man of Ross'.

Left: In the square in front of the Man of Ross is this striking sculpture of leaping salmon, crafted by leading local sculptor Walenty Pytel.

Above: Also facing Walenty Pytel's sculpture is the Swan Hotel, seen here in a fine publicity postcard which was posted in 1905. Clearly the carriages are carefully posed, and bystanders watch the photographer. It is assumed that it is the hotel omnibus that is prominent in the photograph, which features in the advertisement of around 1900 (right).

On the corner of the building, at 1 High Street, is the wine shop of William Pulling & Co. of Hereford. In 1902 it was managed by William Edward Cole. The Swan was built in 1867 as a family, commercial and coaching house and was not of great antiquity as a licensed establishment, and so not to be confused with the earlier Swan and Falcon in High Street. When the Swan was offered for sale in 1914, it was described as having fourteen bedrooms, a billiard room, smoking room, dining room and assembly room. There was stabling for eighty horses as well as a garage for the relatively infrequent motorist. Within a few years it had been taken over by Trust Houses Ltd and eventually closed in the 1980s, to be converted into offices and flats. The name can still be seen in the glass of the canopy over the main entrance.

ROSS.

The Swan Hotel

(OVERLOOKING THE RIVER).

FIRST-CLASS, with MODERATE CHARGES.

LADIES' COFFEE ROOM.

BILLIARDS.

The HOTEL OMNIBUS meets all Trains.

POSTING.

FOR TARIFF AND ROOMS,

ADDRESS,

THE MANAGERESS.

82

Above: The situation of the Hope and Anchor near the river in Ross (photographed in 2001) was to the advantage of the licensees. In the late eighteenth century there was already a victualler here, and no doubt his trade was boosted by hungry and thirsty bargees working on the river. In 1811 a horse towing path was opened, with horses replacing the bow hauliers who had previously towed the barges upriver, so this may have affected his trade. But this was no doubt more than made up for by the increased number of tourists who came to enjoy the acclaimed Wye tour. Of course, it would only be persons of means who could afford both the time and money to make the tour, as reported in the *Hereford Journal* of 5 September 1792:

> On Friday last, his Grace the Duke of Norfolk, accompanied by Mr Howard, Mr Walwyn, Capt, Scudamore, and a party of Ladies, made an excursion in Newton's pleasure boats, down the River Wye, from Ross to Monmouth. – It was their intention to proceed to Chepstow; but owing to the wetness of the weather, they dismissed their boats at Monmouth, and, after taking a view of the town, returned on Saturday to dinner at Holm Lacy.

In the early 1830s William Newton, probably of the same family, opened the Hope and Anchor as a beerhouse, which seems to have closed when he died in 1838. His widow Sarah worked as a basket maker, but had reopened the pub by 1851, also hiring out pleasure boats. A younger William Newton was here by 1859 and died in 1866, when the inn passed out of the family.

Opposite: Henry Dowell and members of his family were here at the beginning of the twentieth century, and he was much associated with the river, as this publicity material shows. Visible is the stern-wheel steam launch *Wilton Castle*, which plied on the river before the First World War.

Now, however, the Hope and Anchor does not rely on the river trade, but uses its pleasant position on the river bank to attract its clientele.

This photograph of the King's Head (left) dates from around 1910, when J.J. Miles was the proprietor, and encapsulates the old and the new. This is one of only two inns in Ross that have been known by the same name since the seventeenth century. It was a coaching inn from the eighteenth century, when the passengers on the 'London and Oxford Flying Coach' could be carried from the King's Head to Oxford for 17s or London for £1 7s. It was also a posting house, where post-chaises could be hired. In 1836 Joseph, the landlord, advertised that he had made arrangements for his clients so that he could 'Post them for ONE SHILLING PER MILE, with excellent and fast horses'. In 1866 James Maddy, the landlord, advertised that the stabling had been expanded to hold 100 horses.

In 1896 it was advertised that a 'bus met all trains' (below). In the 1920s it was taken over by Trust Houses Ltd and completely renovated in 1984. The King's Bar, where real ale is sold, is Georgian, with pine panelling.

KING'S HEAD HOTEL, ROSS.

JAMES MADDY

Takes this opportunity of thanking his friends and the public generally for the kind continued support extended to him over a period of Seventeen years, and begs to intimate to them that he has had the entire ESTABLISHMENT THOROUGHLY RENOVATED, and he confidently hopes that those who may favour him with their support will find every arrangement to their entire satisfaction. He further begs to state that he has INCREASED the OUT-DOOR and YARD ACCOMMODATION, by adding the Swan Yard and Stabling to his own, having now first-class Stables capable of accommodating 100 horses; added thereto every convenience in Horse-boxes, Coach-houses, &c., &c.

THE BILLIARD ROOM

Has undergone entire repairs, the Table equal to new, and every attention will be paid to Visitors, a Marker being present at all times during the day.

A MARKET ORDINARY, as usual, at Two o'Clock on Thursdays.

Posting in all its branches; Hearses, Mourning Coaches, &c., &c. at the shortest notice.

JULY, 1867.

The only surviving inn in the market place at Ross is the Crown and Sceptre, seen here in 2001 (right). Both the building and the name date from the seventeenth century, although the former has received some alterations over the years.

By 1830 Thomas Meredith was here, and was still in charge in 1851 when he was described as a victualler. He was soon succeeded by J.R. Horlick, who advertised his services in 1855. Evidently he was busy, as the business had expanded to take in the wine and spirit trade, as well as brewing beer and providing accommodation. Horlick died shortly after this and his widow carried on the business for a while.

Provision of food (victuals) seems to have been a long-standing service provided by the Crown and Sceptre, and continues to the present day, although the real ale provided is not now brewed on the premises. This publicity post card (below) of a dinner for some unknown event was posted in 1905.

Left: Although there has been a licensed premises on the site of the King Charles II in Broad Street, Ross, since the fourteenth century, its present name is less than 100 years old (photographed in 2001). Its earlier name was the Black Lion, and it was called by that name up until the latter part of the eighteenth century. It then became the business premises of T.W. Purchas, a wine and sprit merchant. Later publicity claimed, slightly doubtfully, that the firm was established in 1790. Purchas was responsible for reconstructing the building above the cellars, which are hewn from the solid rock. Early in the twentieth century this long-established business was taken over by Charles Edwards Ltd. In the 1930s this company opened the King Charles Bar, which eventually became the King Charles II.

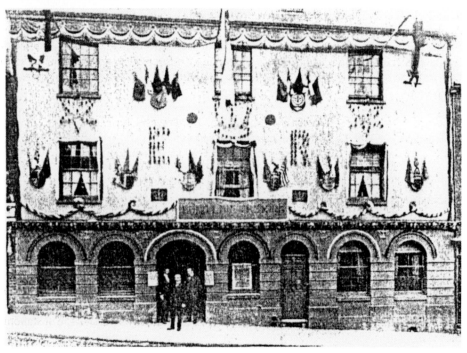

A patriotic display on the front of T.W. Purchas & Sons, for Coronation Day 1902.

M J. R. — B. No 6254

John Kyrle, the 'Man of Ross', lived in the High Street in a fine half-timbered house. After his death his property came down through the family, and about the middle of the century the tenant, James Prosser, a saddler, converted it into an inn called the King's Arms. An attempt to sell the property was made in 1779 but was seemingly unsuccessful as it remained in the family. One visitor to the King's Arms in 1795 was the poet S.T. Coleridge, who composed a poem beginning:

> 'Here dwelt the "Man of Ross!" O Traveller, hear,
> Departed Merit claims a reverent tear!'
> Friend to the friendless, to the sick man health,
> With gen'rous joy he view'd his modest wealth ...'

At that time the licensee was a D. George, who kept several pleasure boats on the river. The last licensee was Charles Witherington, formerly a waiter at the Bell, Gloucester, who took over in 1800, advertising 'BOATS and Refreshments provided for Parties or Excursions down the Romantic River Wye'. He was probably still there when the inn closed in 1805. It may have reopened as the Mitre, as in 1816 'The Mitre Hotel or Man of Ross House' was advertised as being to let. If so, it was not successful and by 1835 the property had been divided into two, Benjamin Powle, a printer, taking the right-hand half. The Powle family was here until at least 1909, and then the premises were occupied by another printer H.C. Jefferies until the *Ross Gazette* took over in 1914. In recent times the *Ross Gazette* moved out, and a firm of stationers moved in.

The Chase Hotel began as a private mansion built in 1818 by a Ross attorney. In the late 1920s it was converted into a hotel, and has since been considerably extended. The original Georgian front can still be seen in this photograph of 2001.

SUN INN,
HIGH-STREET,
ROSS.

JAMES THOMAS WESTON

(Late Porter at Ross Union),

DESIRES to inform the Inhabitants of Ross, and the Public generally, that he has just TAKEN TO THE ABOVE PREMISES, where, on and after April the 8th, he hopes, by supplying

ALES & STOUT,

Of the best quality, to merit a fair share of public patronage.

FIRST-CLASS CIDER ON DRAUGHT.

TOBACCOS and CIGARS of the Finest Brands.

Close to the Man of Ross's House was the short-lived Sun Tavern. For most of the nineteenth century this was a refreshment room, and opened as a beerhouse in 1867-68, a natural extension of this business. A later licensee, James Weston, advertised that he had taken over the Sun Tavern in 1892 with this interesting poster. It closed somewhere around the beginning of the First World War.

The building that was formerly the Sun Tavern can be identified by this fine fire mark, which shows that the building and contents had been insured by Sun Life in 1813. The policy shows that the building itself was insured for £350.

These two photographs of the Lough Pool at Sellack were taken in 1999. Taking its name from a nearby field which, in 1607, was called 'ye Louge Poole', it did not become a beerhouse until 1867, and remained as such until well into the twentieth century before it gained a full licence. In the 1920s it was recorded that the building was 'built in the seventeenth century and has modern additions at either end. Inside the building are some exposed ceiling-beams and the roof is of queen-post type'. Since then there have been further additions to the Lough Pool, and some alterations, but in its essentials the building is the same. The emphasis now is on fine food, for which the inn is well known.

This quiet scene outside the New Harp Inn at Hoarwithy dates from the early years of the twentieth century, when Thomas Dance was the licensee. At that time it was dignified by being called a hotel. The first licensee was James Preece, who had been at the Old Harp in the village, but in 1875 was in court because he had detained property of the Hoarwithy Friendly Society. However, he was still at the Old Harp in 1881 but by the late 1880s this had been bought out and converted to the Harp Temperance Hotel (below, in the early twentieth century). Preece moved to Fishbrook Cottage, which became the New Harp. In 1980 it was reported that once a

week a doctor from Ross conducted his surgery in the bar of the New Harp during which, naturally, the bar was closed. Closed for nearly a year after a fire, the newly refurbished inn offers an unusual cuisine, with regular fish nights, the fish coming from further afield than the river Wye! In 2007 it was the winner of the pub of the year category in the Flavours of Herefordshire competition.

This photograph of the Green Man, Fownhope, dates from the 1920s, and shows the inn before the brickwork was colour-washed. Claimed to date from 1485, it is thought that the present building was built in the seventeenth century on an 'L' shaped plan, with later additions. Its earlier name was the Naked Boy, then it became the Green Man in the eighteenth century. It is the meeting place of the Heart of Oak Society, dating from around 1839 but which had its origins in a Friendly Society founded in 1791. An annual walk is still held.

During the twentieth century the size of the inn was increased from eight bedrooms in 1931 to twenty in 1999. Extensive renovations were carried out in 1948 and improvements have continued so that the inn succeeds in satisfying the needs of the twenty-first century.

Originally built in 1602, the Moon at Mordiford has been an inn since at least the eighteenth century, if not before. This 2001 photograph shows clearly the earlier timbered part of the building, with the later wing in local rubble stone beyond. In 1902 Daniel J. Hughes, the licensee, offered 'Good Accommodation for cyclists, tourists, and fishermen. Good Stabling'. The Moon benefits from its position near to the river and the well-known Mordiford Loop walk. An extension for a restaurant has, in recent years, been constructed out of old timbers to match the main body of the inn.

In 1851 Hampton Bishop was said to contain '...a few detached houses. It is not extensive, and consists mainly of farmers'. There was also the Bunch of Carrots, seen here in a photograph of 2001, which served local needs. Prominent by the inn is the embankment called the Stank, which acts a flood defence for the village. Showing on a map of the 1720s, it was repaired a few years ago. Even then the flood defences proved inadequate in the exceptional floods of July 2007, and the village had to be evacuated. The new landlord, who had only been at the Carrots for six weeks, had to evacuate the pub. Being close to the river, in earlier times the local trade would have been augmented by the passing bargees, but by the middle of the nineteenth century the river trade had virtually finished. In 1858 the landlord was Richard Wheatstone, who may have been one of the Fownhope family of that name, who were connected with the river. The Wheatstone family was here, off and on, until the twentieth century. In 1921 the Carrots was described as being a famous inn, frequented by fishermen, and at that time there was still a ferry across the river. It was also said that many years previously during a flood a boat had floated into the orchard at the Carrots, and that, for many years, this was occupied, upside down, by a tenant, and known as Noah's Ark! However, while some of the present day passing trade for the inn no doubt arrives by water or on foot, most is by car. The inn has developed to cater for this increased trade, with a carvery and restaurant.

Opposite: Dating from the fifteenth century, the Black Swan at Much Dewchurch was converted to an inn during the first part of the eighteenth century. William Sparkes, licensee and victualler at the Black Swan from about 1851 until his death late in 1884, was also a tailor. Perhaps he needed the money, as in 1861 he had eight young children. The following year the Black Swan was offered for sale, and the particulars show that there was then stabling for twelve horses, and also a large Club room about 36ft by 18ft. In 1927 the eminent Woolhope Club visited the Black Swan and much enjoyed analysing the building. Modern approval was given in 2006 by the local branch of CAMRA which stated that it was 'a most interesting and delightful fifteenth century heavily-beamed pub, complete with a priest hole'.

Above: The Black Swan, Much Dewchurch, in the early twentieth century.

Right: The sign for the Black Swan, published in the *Woolhope Club Transactions* in 1960.

The Tump Inn, at Wormelow (above, photographed in 2001), is actually in the parish of Much Birch. Built in 1778 and opened in 1780, it took its name from a tumulus that was across the road, but which was cleared away for road widening in the nineteenth century. This was one of the many pubs in Herefordshire at which cockfighting took place. In 1805 there was an advertisement in the *Hereford Journal* for a cock-match at the inn between the Gentlemen of the Banks of the Munnow and the Gentlemen of the Banks of the Wye. Rather gruesomely, and in the spirit of the times, it promised that 'Good Fighting is expected'.

When the inn was unsuccessfully offered for sale by auction in 1933 (left) it was described as a hotel 'recently modernised throughout' and made a point of a drive-in for cars, even more essential now than then!

PARTICULARS of

A VALUABLE AND ATTRACTIVE MODERN

Freehold Fully Licensed Free House

KNOWN AS

"WORMELOW TUMP HOTEL"

On WEDNESDAY, MAY 10th, 1933.

Situate at WORMELOW, directly opposite Bryngwyn Mansion, on the main Hereford—Monmouth Road and at the cross roads to Allensmore and Ross, 7 Miles from Hereford and Ross, commanding an excellent trade and being a well-known and exceedingly popular house.

The Hotel adjoins the Kennels of the South Herefordshire Hunt and is also a listed R.A.C. house.

The Property, which has a Drive in for cars, is substantially built of Stone and has been recently modernised throughout by the owner.

The Rooms are all light and cheerful, the accommodation being conveniently arranged and comprising :—

    ENTRANCE PASSAGE with Porch ;

    BAR ;

    LARGE SMOKE ROOM fitted with Register Grate and Picture Rail, with door giving access to SNUGGERY ;

    LOUNGE, fitted with modern Register Grate ;

    PRIVATE SITTING ROOM, fitted with Oak Mantelpiece, modern Register Grate and Hot-Water Boiler ;

    SMALL TEA ROOM ;

    KITCHEN, with Stove, Dresser, Glazed Sink and Drainer ;

    STORE ROOM, with Concrete Floor ;

    LARGE CLUB ROOM ;

    FIVE EXCELLENT BEDROOMS and MODERN BATHROOM fitted with Bath, Lavatory Basin and W.C. ;

    GOOD CELLARAGE with Concrete Floor and 2 Skid Ways.

Above: The Cross Keys at Goodrich was on the old turnpike road from Ross to Monmouth, and no doubt derived much of its trade from this. Since 1960 the main road has been diverted away from the centre of the village, but the inn has continued to flourish, although the mounting block, seen here in this photograph taken in 2000, is unlikely to be used much!

Right: This carefully posed photograph of the Hostelrie in Goodrich was taken by Unwin of Hereford, whose name appears in trade directories between 1890 and 1909. Known as the Crown and Anchor in the early eighteenth century, it had closed by 1819 and then was run as a parish workhouse for a few years. By 1832 it had reopened as a beerhouse under its old name. In 1845 it was purchased by Sir Samuel Meyrick of Goodrich Court, and the building was redesigned into its present form, reflecting the Gothic style of Goodrich Court. It then became the Meyrick Arms, but by 1851 it had become the Hostelrie, a name it has born ever since. It has since been extended and is a private hotel, although it also provides for diners and drinkers as well.

Above: The Old Court Hotel, Whitchurch, pictured here about the year 1930 when it was still a private residence, was built in the sixteenth century, possibly incorporating some earlier elements. It was extended in the seventeenth century. In the hands of the Gwillim family from the sixteenth century until 1800, it did not become a hotel until after the Second World War. It has since been much extended, but incorporates many historic features.

Above: This superb photograph of the local hunt, meeting outside the Red Lion, Peterstow, was taken in the 1950s. This inn was built on an 'L' shaped plan in the seventeenth century, and has since been extended. Its position on a minor crossroads was no doubt an advantage, as was the passing traffic on the main road that is now the A49. However, in the nineteenth century the licensees often had other occupations, such as coal dealer in 1858, threshing machine proprietor in 1867, and tiler and plasterer in 1902, so perhaps it was not as prosperous as it might have been. In the late 1970s it was delicensed and became a private residence, as is happening to so many pubs now. Happily, however, in this case it reopened as an inn a number of years later.

Opposite below: The name of the Olde Ferrie at Symonds Yat West calls attention to the ferry that still operates here. In this 1930s photograph the flat-bottomed ferry can be seen tied up against the bank below the inn. Housed in a building that is claimed to date from the fifteenth century, it has the curiosity of a right of way through the pub buildings down a flight of steps. Since the eighteenth century Symonds Yat has been a magnet for tourists, and even in the 1920s the restaurant at the Olde Ferrie Inn could seat 200 diners, facilities that continue to this day, with superb river views.

HEREFORDSHIRE.

Much Birch, Little Birch and Kingstone.

Valuable FREE PUBLIC HOUSE and FREEHOLD PROPERTIES.

Messrs. HILES - SMITH & SON

will offer the following Lots for SALE BY AUCTION, at

The Law Society's Hall, East Street, Hereford,

On Wednesday, 26th November, 1919,

at **THREE** o'clock in the Afternoon, subject to Conditions of Sale to include the Common Form Conditions of the Herefordshire Incorporated Law Society.

Lot 1. All that Freehold Fully-licensed Inn, known as

"THE AXE & CLEAVER"

situate in the Parish of Much Birch on the Main Road between Hereford and Ross.

The house contains bar, tap-room, smoke-room, parlour, kitchen, 5 bedrooms, beer-cellar and offices; the outside buildings comprise club-room, stabling, barn, cider-house and cow-house; with garden, grass paddock and orchard, the whole containing about

TWO ACRES

This is one of the Oldest-Established Licensed Houses in the district, and is an ancient picturesque hostelry.

The house is Free and a good business has been carried on for many years, and is now in the occupation of Mr. Walter Brewer as a Yearly Tenant.

Tithe 10/11,

From the roadside, the Axe and Cleaver at Much Birch appears to be a complete 1930s rebuild, but that is not so. This old publicity postcard (opposite above), dating from the 1920s, shows its seventeenth-century origins. The first mention of the Axe and Cleaver is in 1851, when John Jones, a farmer, was also running this beerhouse. It was sold by auction in 1888, when it was described as an 'old-established and fully licensed public house'. It was again offered for sale in 1919 (above), when the brewers Godsall & Son acquired the premises, and the sale particulars of the building illustrated here give a good description at this time. In the 1920s E.C. Pugh was the tenant, and on the back of the postcard described above it is stated that it was a 'Free house. All beers drawn from the Wood. Wines and Spirits of superior quality. ACCOMMODATION FOR MOTORISTS, CYCLISTS, AERONAUTS, &c. TEAS AND LUNCHEONS PROVIDED. WELL-AIRED BEDS. GOOD STABLING'. It would be interesting to know how many passing aeronauts dropped in! From about 1930 the inn was owned by the Stroud Brewery, and in the late 1930s was rebuilt as we see it today. Now it benefits from its roadside position, with a restaurant, caravan and camping facilities. There is also a regular bus service past the door, so there is no need to get the car out to visit.

Above: A 1920s publicity postcard for the Axe and Cleaver.

Right: The terms at the Axe and Cleaver in the 1950s seem remarkably cheap today!

A.A., R.A.C.
APPOINTED

Axe & Cleaver Inn

MUCH BIRCH
HEREFORD

Proprietor:
E. H. WHEATSTONE

Telephone
WORMELOW 3

A FULLY-LICENSED old-world country Inn delightfully modernized. Situated in beautiful country half-way between Hereford and Ross. Ideal for walking or as a centre while touring the WYE VALLEY. On a good 'bus route with an hourly service each way. All bedrooms are very well appointed with h. & c. water, Slumberland beds, and electric fires.

There is a very cosy Lounge and pleasant Dining Room. Excellent cuisine and every comfort—ideal for Winter residents.

A nice garden and grass tennis court are at the disposal of patrons.

Good hunting country with South Hereford Hounds and Ross Harriers. Riding can be arranged locally by appointment in advance.

Garage for 6 cars. Petrol and Service Station 50 yards.

TERMS.

Per week : 5½ guineas each inclusive.

Per day : 17/6 (minimum 4 days).

Hot Baths, 1/-. Garage free.

Bed and Breakfast : 10/6 each.

Dinner 4/6. Luncheon 3/6 to 4/6. Afternoon Teas 1/6 to 2/-. Sandwiches and Snacks can be obtained at the Bar at reasonable charges during opening hours, 10.30 to 2.30 and 6 till 10.

Patrons can have packed meals if they wish to go out for the day.

The contrast between the above photograph of Harewood End Inn, taken at the beginning of the twenty-first century, and the postcard of around 1935 (below) is dramatic. While the inn has been tidied up, the road has changed out of all recognition. Would that the main road from Hereford to Ross was like this now! The postcard shows only a single car outside and a steam traction engine opposite the inn. There has been an inn here since the seventeenth century, although the present building is not as old as that. Up to the middle of the nineteenth century the magistrates met every other week here, but after a new police station was opened nearby, moved to a specially constructed magistrates' room there. In the twenty-first century the inn benefits from the good access of its roadside position, and the catering for small parties, advertised in 1931, has expanded, as the roadside barn has now been converted to a restaurant and function room.

The relatively modern extension to the Bull Ring in Kingstone draws attention away from the lower, earlier, part of the building which was built in the seventeenth century. The name was taken from the bull ring, which was where bull-baiting and bear-baiting took place, the last occasion being in 1815. Already an alehouse in the mid-eighteenth century, and likely before that, this was another venue for the 'sport' of cock fighting, matches being advertised to take place here in 1793 and 1796. When it was advertised as being for let late in 1821, it was stated that 16 acres of ground went with it. At that time the tenant was Thomas Preece, although his wife Mary seems to have been the licensee. Early in 1822 Thomas Preece's farming stock and furniture were sold by auction, so it seems he may have been in financial difficulties.

By 1851 the Bull Ring was being run by Frederick Seall, a member of a local family, whose main trade was that of a tailor. He may have run that business from the shop that was on the left-hand side of the present front door. After his death in the 1862, his wife carried on until the late 1870s, assisted by her son (another Fredrick), and she then lived in retirement until her death in 1894 at the age of eighty-five. The shop seems to have closed in the early years of the twentieth century.

In the early part of the twentieth century the annual May Fair was held here for three days and the swings and roundabouts were erected in the orchard behind the Bull Ring. Later in the twentieth century the telephone came to Kingstone and Jack Meek, landlord of the Bull Ring by 1937, had one of the earlier ones (T.N. Madley 35). The Bull Ring continues to adapt to changing circumstances, and in 2004 it underwent a face-lift, reopening in the summer after the first phase of refurbishment.

This delightful photograph of the Red Lion, Madley, dating from the early years of the twentieth century, reflects a more tranquil past. A timber-framed building dating from the seventeenth century, the façade has been rebuilt in brick. Certainly a public house in the eighteenth century, if not before, in 1775 a Main of Cocks (a cock-fighting match) was advertised to take place here. John Marsh, a landlord who died in 1793, was known for his bare-knuckle boxing – no Queensbury Rules then. (Derek Foxton Collection)

By the time that this photograph was taken in 2005 the texture of the brick front had been lost by being painted over. However, the building in general and the bar in particular have not been spoilt. The bar still retains its flagstone floor, and would be immediately recognisable to the customers and publicans of a hundred years ago.

Apart from the signs on the wall, this modern photograph of the Red Lion at Bredwardine could have been taken any time in the last hundred years or more. Indeed, the Red Lion has changed very little since it was built early in the eighteenth century. The size of the inn comes as a surprise in what is now a relatively quiet place, but as late as the early part of the nineteenth century the road from Hereford which crossed Bredwardine bridge was the main road to Brecon via Hay. The tolls for crossing Bredwardine bridge paid for its upkeep. Bredwardine was also on a drovers' route from Wales, and there was a pound for sheep and cattle near the bridge. The drovers no doubt had an overnight stop at the Red Lion.

The Red Lion was also a centre of village life, and glimpses are given in the diaries of the Revd Francis Kilvert, who was rector of Bredwardine in the 1870s. On 10 December 1878 he recorded a meeting here of the trustees of Bredwardine bridge, where the tolls of the bridge were let for £35. Also, this was where the Petty Sessions were held, the magistrates meeting on the first Friday of the month. The room they used was furnished by the landlord, and when John Langford became insolvent in 1870, the contents of the magistrates' room were included in an inventory and valuation of his effects. The old courtroom is now the Leapers' Bar, where those that enjoy the fishing that the hotel offers can meet and tell fishermen's tales about the one that got away!

At the upper end of the Golden Valley is Dorstone, which is served by the Pandy Inn. This photograph of the inn was taken around 1904 and the building is essentially the same today, although with tiles instead of slates. While stories of its antiquity are open to question, it was certainly a public house in the eighteenth century when the present building was constructed. Indeed, there are physical clues apart from the name that suggest it began life as a fulling mill – known as a pandy – before it was licensed. At the heart of the village, up until the last third of the nineteenth century there were annual fairs for horned cattle, horses, sheep and pigs which took place on the village green outside the inn.

LOT 16.

An Old Established Fully Licensed and Highly Popular Free House

KNOWN AS

"THE PANDY INN"

practically the only house of call within a road radius of about 3 miles. Situate in the Village of Dorstone within 5 minutes of Station. The accommodation represents Entrance Passage through to back, Tap Room with Bar, Sitting Room, Club Room, Spirit Store, Private Sitting Room, Kitchen with Baking Oven, and good Cellar having yard approach. Above are large Landing, 4 good Bedrooms, Bathroom, Box and Servants Bedrooms. In close proximity to the House are Dairy, 3-Stall Cart Stable and Coach House with Lofting over, 2 Piggeries with yards, Open Wainhouse, and Cowhouse for 3. There is an excellent supply of water to the premises, and the area, which includes a valuable though small Orchard, represents

0a. 2r. 36p. (or thereabouts).

For many years past this house has been in the occupation of Mr. G. Probert on yearly Candlemas taking at an arranged Rental as between Owner and Tenant.

The commuted Tithe Rent charges amount to 3s. 5d., and the Land Tax to 2s. 10d.

The Pandy belonged to a local estate, which at the beginning of the twentieth century was owned by the local rector. Outlying portions of the estate were sold off by auction in 1919, the sale details printed here giving a good description of it at that time. At the auction it was bought by Ephraim Pikes, the local blacksmith, who ran it for a short while, giving it up because it interfered with his other business.

Now it serves food as well as beer, and in deference to the number of workers from the EU, includes Polish dishes on its menu.

More or less in the centre of the Golden Valley is Peterchurch and the Boughton Arms. This photograph of the inn was taken soon after the First World War, at a time when traffic was rather less than it is now (above). There is little difference in the Boughton Arms in the second photograph, taken some eighty years later (below), except that the brickwork has been painted over and the redundant mounting block has been removed. This inn was named after the Boughton family, landowners in the valley until the middle of the nineteenth century. In the eighteenth century cock fighting used to be held in the field behind the Boughton Arms. For a period of about 100 years, there were only three different names above the door. From at least 1818 until 1861 members of the Gwyn family held the licence. William Garrett came next and he was here for about thirty years, calling it a 'hotel' and advertising the delights of fishing in the area. His successor as proprietor, James Thomas junior. lasted well into the twentieth century. In the latter's time Robert Jones V.C., who met an untimely death in 1898, was one of the regulars at the inn. Now, with current legislation, in 2007 an application was made for a smoking shelter for use in conjunction with the Boughton Arms. This was approved, but with conditions.

Above: At the lower end of the Golden Valley is the world-famous Dore Abbey, the truncated remains of a monastic church, still in use as a parish church. This building attracts many visitors each year, but the parish of Abbey Dore does not have any licensed premises to refresh them, the old Red Lion having closed nearly 150 years ago. However, not far down the road from Dore Abbey is the Neville Arms, just over the border in the civil parish of Ewyas Harold. This had its origins in the old Griffin Inn, which seems to have opened in the 1860s when it was run by James Edwards, a carpenter, and after his death in 1883, by his widow, who was still there at the beginning of the twentieth century. This was part of the estate of the Marquess of Abergavenny, and in 1910 was tenanted by John Gwillim. Soon afterwards the Neville Arms was built on the south side of the Griffin, and William Thomas Morgan took over. He was still there in January 1920 when the estate was sold by auction and the sale particulars noted that 'The Bath and Fittings, also the Bell Fittings, are the property of the tenant'. No doubt the plumbing is now a permanent feature of the inn since bed and breakfast accommodation is now offered! In 2004 a new restaurant was opened, called the Dore River Restaurant.

Opposite above: This recent photograph of the Cornewall Arms, Clodock, shows a scene that has altered little since it was built in the eighteenth century, adjoining – and indeed almost in – the churchyard. The name was given to the inn because it belonged to the Moccas estate of the Cornewall family, and records show that William Lewis, landlord from the late 1860s, paid an annual rent of £13 6s 8d. As a result of a scandal in 1893 the Cornewall Arms was closed, and then sold to an Evesham brewery. It reopened the following year. Little has changed at the Cornewall Arms since before the Second World War, and in 2006 CAMRA described it as 'a tiny unspoilt pub of great character'. The lounge area is just like someone's front room!

Above: The Crown Inn, Longtown, which dates from 1751, was probably an inn from the start. For a few years from 1894 the Crown was owned and run by Benjamin Price. About 1900 he moved up the road to become a tenant at the New Inn, leaving a tenant in the Crown, which he owned! In charge for some fifteen years from 1973, Ian Brymer restored and modernised the Crown, with inside toilets and a porch to help solve the problems of surface water – when the drains in the road outside were blocked, the water came in the front door and out at the back! Subsequently the inn has had a chequered history, but it has now been newly refurbished and offers well-recommended accommodation to visitors.

The star of this early twentieth century photograph of road surfacing outside the Temple Bar at Ewyas Harold is undoubtedly the Aveling Porter road roller. The audience to the rear seem to be enjoying the spectacle, or maybe just wanted to be photographed! At that period the Temple Bar was relatively new, having become licensed in the 1850s, a Mrs Ellery being the first landlady. At the time of the photograph, the landlord was Alfred Prosser, baker, corn dealer, and farmer, who sold Arnold, Perrett, & Co.'s Gold Medal Ales & Stout, from the City Brewery, Hereford.

At the time that this photograph was taken around 1900, what is now the Dog Inn at Ewyas Harold was called the Castle Inn, after the pre-Conquest castle just up the road, the earthworks of which remain. Thomas Prosser was the publican at this time, and it is possible that he is the gentleman standing in the doorway. In 2007 the landlord ran foul of the anti-smoking legislation with which he strongly disagreed. He was hauled into court, receiving a fine of £1,075 and had to meet whopping costs of £10,807! On a happier note, in November 2008 it was reported that a black-and-white cob called Murphy was a regular at this inn, and preferred real ale, although despite his name, he did not like Guinness!

This evocative photograph of the Bridge Inn, Michaelchurch Escley, was taken before the First World War. This is the only one of several pubs in the area to have survived. Its immediate predecessor was the Sun Inn, directly opposite the church, which closed around 1870 when the Bridge Inn opened. Pedestrian access to the inn was by the footbridge over the Escley brook, but any wheeled traffic had to negotiate the ford by the side of the footbridge.

Apart from the eye-catching plastic chairs, and the creeper which cloaks the Bridge Inn in this photograph of 2005, there is little change from the earlier photograph, Not seen in the photograph is the road bridge that replaced the ford in 1976 to give better access to the pub's picnic and camp site. As a consequence of the outbreak of foot-and-mouth disease in 2001/2002, the trade was adversely affected and the inn was sold in May 2002. It was sold again in April 2005 for £375,000, but stability has now returned.

It is remarkable that the Bull's Head, Craswall (top) should survive and flourish in such a remote spot, but it does! The interior of the bar has been little altered since the above photograph was taken in 1998, when the pub had just changed hands, and the bar is one of the unique features of the pub. What has changed is the fare on offer, as up to the change of ownership in 1997, all that was on offer was bread, cheese and pickles. A far cry from the extensive menu on offer today!

The Bull's Head seems to have had its origins in the 1820s, when it was called Forest House, soon changed to the present name. For most of its existence it has been a small establishment, with the licensees deriving part of their income – probably the major part – from farming. Things only changed after Beattie Lewis retired in 1997, when the pub was sold. She had run it with her husband for forty-four years. The Bull's Head was gradually renovated and accommodation provided within the existing building without losing its character, the bar being left unspoilt.

6

KINGTON AND NORTH-WEST HEREFORDSHIRE

The rather grand front of the Burton Hotel, Mill Street, Kington,
in the 1950s, when traffic was not the problem that it is today.

The Olde Tavern at Sunset, Kington, is in a time warp, recognized by an entry in CAMRA's guide to good pub interiors. Claimed to have been established in 1767 when it was known as the House in the Fields, it was certainly in existence in the mid-nineteenth century, when it was called the Railway Tavern. It still has the stables that were used by horses, for it was a horse-drawn tramway after which the tavern was named, which reached Kington in 1822. In the 1860s the Railway Tavern was held by Richard Griffiths, and then his son Thomas, but by 1881 it had been taken over by the curiously named Shadrach Morris. In the early 1880s the licensee was Alfred Jones, who also owned the premises, and advertised that he sold wines, spirits and cigars, and the noted home-brewed ales – brewed by himself, of course! In 1920 there was a proposal to refurbish the premises, but this never came about. In 1926 the glass sign for Ye Olde Tavern cracked and was taken down. The pace of life is slow at this excellent inn – the sign was not put up again until 1985! About 1930 Alfred was succeeded by Frederick Jones, and then sisters Gertrude and Mary Jones. In 1972 the sisters were interviewed on television, and reminisced about brewing their own beer, opening during two world wars, and told about being asked for a 'dog's nose', which turned out to be gin with a dash of beer. The sisters died in 1976 and 1989 respectively. Now the inn remains unspoilt, and still contains many curios and the plans for the refurbishment that did not come about. Now the brewery tap for real ale brewed by the owners, it was CAMRA's Herefordshire Pub of the Year in 2004 and Area Pub of the year in 2005. In recent years the facilities have been extended by the addition of a bistro.

By the 1930s the motoring age had really arrived at the Oxford Arms in Duke Street, Kington, recommended by both the RAC and the AA. Formerly called the Salutation, in 1745 it was let at an annual rent of £16 10s. The change of name to the Oxford Arms is not surprising, as it was owned by the Earl of Oxford. Probably at this time the building was re-fronted, for behind the thin brick façade is a timber-framed building. In 1776 there was a diligence, from the Oxford Arms to the Green Dragon, Hereford. By 1781 a diligence set out for London from the Oxford Arms, which took two days to reach the capital. Thomas Rogers, a landlord in the early part of the nineteenth century, also rented the King's Arms, the other large inn at the time, farmed, and was an auctioneer. Because of bankruptcy, in May 1838 most of his goods were sold by order of the sheriff and he left the Oxford Arms and King's Head, but carried on as an auctioneer. In July 1847 Rogers was found guilty of forgery, and was sentenced to three months imprisonment and then to be transported for twenty years. Unlike Rogers, the Oxford Arms continued to flourish and in 1847 a new assembly room was opened. In 1867 the licensee retired and the Oxford Arms was advertised as being to let, with or without 55 acres of land. It was stated that the house was empty, and needed refurnishing, 'Parties treating should have the command of from £1,200 to £1,500'. It was taken by William Harvey, who subsequently bought the Oxford Arms, and after his death in the 1890s, his widow Mary ran it for a short time before she retired. Much work was done on the building in 1937, and the 1939 *Hereford Guide* described it as having been 'entirely redecorated and refurnished' with a 'beautiful Dining and Visitors' Lounge'. In recent years it has a somewhat chequered career, with long periods of closure.

Left: A small group of people are gathered outside the Wine Vaults, in High Street, Kington, at the end of the twentieth century. In the eighteenth century it was named the Fleece. However, by 1840 it had been taken over by John Welson, a wine and spirit merchant, and as a result became known as the Wine Vaults. By 1881 Charles Adams had taken over the business from the Welson family, but in 1891 the premises were vacant. Subsequently the business was run by William Wishlade, who advertised as a wholesale wine and spirit merchant, and rented the building from J.R. Blair of Ramornie, Kington. This use as a wine and spirits dealer continued well into the twentieth century, but in the 1930s it was referred to as the 'Wine Vaults P.H.', so the retail side had taken over! In 1993 it suffered an unfortunate name change to the Old Fogey, but this has now been reversed, reverting to its much older – and nicer – name. In 2006 CAMRA delightfully described it as 'a small, quaint, no frills one-bar drinkers' pub. The atmosphere is very convivial'.

BURTON HOUSE, KINGTON.

THOMAS BOWEN

HAVING purchased those large and commodious premises hitherto known as "Milner's Hotel," begs to inform the Nobility, Gentry, Clergy, and Inhabitants of the town and neighbourhood of Kington, that he intends carrying on the WINE and SPIRIT TRADE in all its branches, in connexion with the ALE and PORTER TRADE, and trusts, by strict personal attention, to merit a continuance of those favours which have always been so liberally bestowed upon him.

As T. B. will purchase all Wines and Spirits for Cash, he will be enabled to go to the best Markets, and supply his friends upon the best terms.

T. B. begs at the same time to intimate his intention of keeping "The Public Hall" open for Assemblies' Balls, Concerts, Public Auctions, Meetings, &c., for the accommodation of the town.

N.B.—AGENT FOR THE CROWN LIFE INSURANCE COMPANY.

January, 1862.

Opposite below: There were no problems parking on either side of the street in this 1950s photograph of the Burton House Hotel, in Mill Street. The secondary pillared portico is the entrance to the public hall associated with the hotel. On the right is the market hall, built in the 1880s on the site of the old King's Head Inn. In 1848, John M. Milner took over his late father's wine and spirits business, opening the premises as a proper hotel in 1851. He also built the public hall, officially opened with a public dinner on 4 November 1856. In 1859, in order to further his career as an auctioneer, he relinquished the hotel and wine and spirit business to Thomas Goreley from Milford Haven. After Goreley sold up at the end of 1861, Thomas Bowen bought the premises, advertising this in the *Hereford Times* (above). He gave up the hotel business, part of the premises being used for the wine and spirits business, and the other as a wine vaults. Bowen sold up the business in 1874, after one failed attempt to do so in 1867. The next two landlords died suddenly, one in 1877 and his successor in 1879. Frank Parmeter, a later landlord, was declared bankrupt in 1891, so the Burton Arms may have been seen as unlucky!

The hotel was sold about 1950, the particulars extolling the location, and stated that six of the twelve bedrooms on the third floor were fitted with washbasins! The photograph of the coffee room at the Burton House Hotel (top) was taken at about this time. Now the Burton Hotel has been brought up-to-date with the facilities that are expected in the twenty-first century, and the adjoining part has been developed as a health spa where visitors to the hotel can further relax.

Above: This happy scene outside the Royal Oak, Church Street, was probably photographed on a market day in the 1920s. An early establishment, it has been developed over the years. When William Evans took over from Thomas Scandrett in 1807, he claimed that 'Great Improvements in the House and Stables have already been made, and still greater are intended...'. Evans relinquished the Royal Oak in 1830, and his successor, George Westall, was declared bankrupt in 1834. Others were more successful, and Thomas Powell, who was here by 1876, was still here in 1903. During his time Sunday drinking in Wales was banned, and so the sign illustrated here would have had some point. At the beginning of the twenty-first century the Royal Oak, discreetly modernised, continues to offer accommodation as it has done for a very long time.

Opposite above: On the opposite side the road from the Royal Oak is the Swan Hotel, seen here in a typical 1960s advertisement. When it was advertised for sale by auction in 1832 it was described as 'That old-established and well-accustomed INN and PUBLIC-HOUSE, called the UPPER SWAN, with good Stabling, Coach-house, extensive Yards, Gardens and Pig-market attached'. At that time it was called the Upper Swan to distinguish it from the Lower Swan in High Street, a distinction that was not needed after the latter closed in 1841 and a tenant could not be found to take it on. The (Upper) Swan continues to dispense hospitality, while its former namesake is now used as shop premises.

Opposite below: Behind the stone façade of the Talbot, Bridge Street, Kington, photographed in 1999, there is a timber-framed building. In the seventeenth century it was called the Lyon and occupied by Philip Holman, High Sheriff of Herefordshire. According to tradition, in 1633 King Charles I slept here. Later the name was changed to the White Talbot, to distinguish it from the Red Talbot, just over the road. The adjective was dropped some time after the Red Talbot closed in 1772. In 1845 it was said that the Talbot had been dilapidated, so perhaps the re-fronting in stone dates from that time. At the beginning of the twentieth century the Talbot was called a hotel, like so many other inns at this time. There has also been a recent change, for the Talbot is now the Lion, approximating to its original name.

In this photograph, taken in 2000, the exterior of the Royal George, Lyonshall, is covered with render, but underneath is a timber-framed building. This is the only surviving licensed premises in Lyonsall, and has a long history, although it is not known when it became an inn. In November 1795 it was advertised that the George Inn at Lyonshall was to be auctioned at the King's Head, Kington, together with 7 acres of land. At that time William Tranter was running the George. A hint about the origin of the name occurs in 1819, when furniture was advertised to be sold 'in the GREAT ROOM, at the House of Mr James Evans, known by the Sign of the George and Dragon'. James Evans was at the George until at least 1828. Sarah Kinnersley, a later landlady, was in charge by 1846, when a new Lodge of the Wolverhampton Order of Odd Fellows was opened at the George. This was in direct competition with a lodge of the Independent Order of Odd Fellows, Manchester Unity, that had been formed at the Greyhound Inn, Lyonshall, in 1844. Sarah Kinnersley was here for at least twenty years, and also traded as a boot and shoemaker. In the 1890s George Cowles took over, but he was not here long and his widow Mary took over the licence after he died. By this time the inn was owned by the Alton Court Brewery of Ross and was called the George Hotel. George Henry Cowles succeeded his mother in the years before the First World War. After the Second World War the name was changed to the Royal George, and in 1961 publicity material made great play of the fact that the inn had been modernised and that there was hot and cold water in all bedrooms.

Opposite above: The Stagg's Head at Titley (photographed in 2000) has had a chequered history. At the beginning of the nineteenth century, it was called the Balance Inn. In 1833 William Greenley of Titley Court bought the inn for £550, and the name was changed to the Stag's Head. The building was also re-fronted in brick, and a grocery and butcher's shop added. William Greenly installed William Palfrey as landlord, no doubt as a reward for nearly twenty years service as coachman to the Greenly family. However, Palfrey died in January 1835, only three weeks after his master. Curiously, the newspaper report incorrectly calls the inn the Buck's Head!

It seems to have been in the later 1870s that the Stag's Head was closed, apparently because there was too much drunkenness and rowdyism on a Sunday, and it did not open again as licensed premises until the 1960s. At that time David Forbes, of Titley Court, purchased the second pint, as he did in 1998 when the inn reopened with new landlords. It is now referred to as the Stagg Inn & Resturant, and the restaurant is internationally famous.

The Greyhound, Pembridge, is seen here covered in render in the 1920s, but it has now been stripped naked. The building is of considerable antiquity as its main block has been dated to the second half of the fifteenth century, with a slightly later cross-wing. John Parry, the licensee during the first half of the nineteenth century, also raised livestock, and in February sold a pig which weighed 7cwt 3qrs (over 350 kg). When he died in 1848 the obituary in the *Hereford Journal* stated that he 'was a man much respected for his honest, open, kind-hearted disposition, and for his general uprightness of conduct'. His widow kept the Greyhound until her own death at the age of eighty-five in June 1867, and it was said that she had been landlady for nearly fifty years. The Greyhound closed as an inn many years ago, but reopened in recent years as the King's House, primarily a restaurant.

Left: Delivering a hogshead at the New Inn, Pembridge, in the late nineteenth century. The location can be identified from the pendant at the corner of the building.

Opposite above: In 1804 James Wathen produced this charming sketch of the New Inn, Pembridge, describing it as 'Cooke's public house'. At that time this early seventeenth-century building had a large porch, and dormer windows in the roof, all long gone. It was called the New Inn in the late eighteenth century, and no doubt well before that. However, in 1802 land was advertised to be sold by auction 'at the house of John Cook, Sun Inn, Pembridge', and this may have been another alternative name (or even a mistake!). In 1807 the New Inn was advertised to be sold by auction, being then let for the low rent of £14. The following year John Caldwell was licensee, but it is not sure if he bought the property or merely rented it. John Caldwell, his widow Elizabeth, and son Joseph, held the New Inn in succession until about 1850, and it is clear that it was at the heart of the village. Thus the local Association for Prosecution of Felons for Pembridge, Eardisland, Shobdon, Staunton-on-Arrow and Lyonshall, met at the New Inn, and when races were held in Pembridge the 'ordinary' was held at the New Inn. Tithe payments were made here, the Petty Sessions were held here, and after the Pembridge ploughing match was held in 1838, the report in the *Hereford Journal* said that a 'sumptuous dinner' was provided by Mrs Caldwell. John Chandler, here by the mid-1880s, was still licensee in 1914 as a tenant of J.C. Charlton Parr, Esq. of Staunton Park, Staunton-on-Arrow. Photographs show that in Chandler's time the New Inn looked much as it does today (below, in the 1960s). Such a large building has clearly had many alterations over the years, and in 1952 it was reported that three fireplaces had been uncovered during renovations. However, the New Inn has kept its character, and the pleasant, slightly old-fashioned interior makes a welcome change.

This charming photograph of the Unicorn, Weobley, taken around 1890, depicts a peaceful scene (below). This inn had been opened by 1809 when William Lloyd was tenant. His widow Jane took over about 1830, and by 1841 she had been succeeded by their daughter Mary Ann Lloyd, who ran it until the 1870s when she retired. By 1876 Edwin Garrett, a timber merchant, had taken over, followed by William Watkins in the 1880s. He was evidently very busy, although some aspects of his work were probably not too popular, for he not only ran the pub but was also a beer agent, assistant overseer, and assessor and collector of taxes!

By 1890 the Unicorn was owned and run by William Jones, who was also a nail manufacturer. His wife was a member of the Powell family who had been nailers in Weobley for several generations. His son John Jones had taken over by 1909, the year in which his father died, and held the licence until his own death in 1951. The reference to the inn being established in 1887 in this publicity of around 1950 probably refers to when William Jones took over the licence (above).

This delightful sketch of the Salutation Inn, Weobley, (right) was made by H. Thornill Timmins in 1891 and except for the loss of the trellis-work porch little has changed, as the modern photograph shows (below). It is made up of several buildings, one of which was constructed of oak felled in the summer of 1583. It was described as an alehouse in the eighteenth century, but this lapsed and it was revived as a beerhouse under the 1830 Act. William Brown, a Scotsman who was licensee in the 1850s and 1860s, bought the property in 1863 and the next year unsuccessfully tried to obtain a spirits licence, which he did not get until two years later. After William Brown's death in the early 1870s, his widow Jane ran

the inn for about ten years. The ownership remained in the family, for when James Smith was licensee in the early twentieth century, it was owned by Mr W. Brown, who was unfortunately an inmate at Burghill Lunatic Asylum. Harriet Smith, James's widow, succeeded him in about 1914, and was still there in 1941. In recent years, the Salutation has been developed as a very successful eating place, as well as a traditional hostelry.

The Morris Dancers in front of the Tram Inn, Eardisley, were photographed in the 1950s (top), but no doubt such a scene occurred many times in the building's long history. It was originally constructed in the second decade of the sixteenth century but may not have become an inn until the mid-eighteenth century. Its earlier name is not known, but in 1818 the tram road from Hay to Eardisley opened, and from this time it was known as the Tram Inn. James Watkins purchased the Tram Inn for £395 in 1847, and he was succeeded as licensee by his widow Ellen, and then daughter, also Ellen. In 1891, because of financial problems, she had to sell the Tram Inn but remained as landlady, paying a rent of £30 per annum. She had married James Baird in 1890, and he later became landlord. After his death in 1901 she took over the licence again, and managed to buy back the inn in 1918. She lived all her life at the Tram Inn, and died there in 1939 at the age of seventy-five.

The Tram Inn was the home of the mythical fox pie. During the Second World War, Lord Haw-Haw's propaganda broadcasts from Germany (middle), claimed that the English were starving, and that the inhabitants of Herefordshire were reduced to eating fox pie! An idea took hold and the Tram Inn would include the mythical fox on its menu, and hold an annual fox-pie supper! This celebrated meal continued for several years after the war, and was revived in 1959 by Gordon and Phyllis Parker, the then licensees (bottom left) and caused much interest and publicity. But Phyllis Parker would never reveal what was in the pie!

Directly opposite the Tram Inn is the New Inn which has played a prominent part in the life of Eardisley since the middle of the eighteenth century (top). In 1798 the Eardisley Friendly Society, which met at the New Inn, adopted a long set of rules, which were printed in 1818. This photograph of around 1900 shows a meeting of the Ancient Order of Druids Benefit Club carefully posed outside the New Inn. In 1901 the building caught fire, and although the livestock and furniture were saved, the building was gutted (above). Fortunately the insurance

paid for the new building that rose from the ashes. In the early 1970s the name was changed to The Mountie, but it has now become the New Strand, and operates as a second-hand book shop, coffee house and licensed bar (above right, in 1999).

Left: Sale particulars of 1965.

Above: The Portway Inn, Staunton-on-Wye is hidden under a covering of ivy in this photograph, taken around 1900. There is no clue as to the identity of the group carefully posed in front of the inn, but it may well include Mrs Emma Williams, landlady at that period. In the past it has also been referred to as the Three Horse Shoes and the Talbot, but the present name really refers to its location.

In the early 1790s the grounds of Garnons, then owned by Sir John Geers Cotterell and to which estate the Portway belonged, were remodelled. Such was the power of a local landowner, that the old turnpike road, along the line of the old Roman road which passed close to the main house, was diverted further south. To the west, the new road joined the old road near the Portway, which still benefited from the passing traffic and so continued to flourish. The Baker family was at the Portway by 1796, if not before, and Elizabeth, the last member of the family to hold the licence, died in 1880 at the age of eighty-two. She must have been a formidable lady, as she also farmed up to 100 acres as well as running the inn.

Somewhere about the year 1800, in William Baker's time, about forty horses' skulls were placed under the floor to help with resonance during musical occasions, supposedly by order of Sir John Geers Cotterell Bart, owner of the Garnons estate. These were rediscovered in 1879, when the inn was rebuilt, and in 1993, during further renovations, a casket containing a horse's skull and a note of the discoveries in 1879 was found. The final skull was found in 2006 and is now displayed under a glass cover, surely unique!

Opposite: Strategically placed on the Welsh border, the Rhydspence Inn, Brilley, (photographed in the 1960s) served the drovers who passed this way on the journey into England, a trade that finally ceased in the mid-nineteenth century. The earliest part of this splendid timber-framed building dates from the early sixteenth century. From time to time the position of the Welsh border seems to have varied and in the early nineteenth century the Rhydspence was licensed in Radnorshire, although it should have been licensed through Herefordshire. In 1863 the house was insured for £250, the cider mill and cider-house for £30, and the barn etc. for £120, rather different to today's figures.

Up to the 1950s the innkeepers were also farmers, but then the land was sold off and the forge subsequently converted into a bar. In recent years the inn was extended to provide more accommodation and the Rhydspence is now a modern hotel and restaurant.

Other local titles published by The History Press

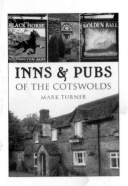

Inns & Pubs of the Cotswolds
MARK TURNER

Taking in all manner of establishments such as the Coach & Horses, an old village pub in Longborough, to the White Hart Royal Hotel, a sixteenth-century inn in Moreton-in-Marsh, the author visits a huge variety of pubs that have made the Cotswolds the delightful area they are today. It is sure to appeal to those who live in the Cotswolds and also to visitors wishing to tour the area's charming pubs.

978 0 7524 4465 9

Birmingham Pubs
KEITH TURNER

This beautiful collection by local expert Keith Turner celebrates the history of Birmingham's numerous pubs, inns, breweries, beers and alehouses. With many archive photographs, entertaining stories of famous landlords and customers and the full history of each establishment, this book will delight anyone with an interest in the history of brewing - and drinking - in the area.

978 0 7524 1809 4

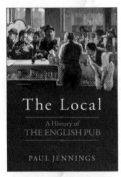

The Local: A History of the English Pub
PAUL JENNINGS

Paul Jennings traces the history of the British pub, and looks at how it evolved from the eighteenth century's coaching inns and humble alehouses, back-street beer houses and 'fine, flaring' gin palaces to the drinking establishments of the twenty-first century. Covering all aspects of pub life, this fascinating history looks at pubs in cities and rural areas, seaports and industrial towns. From music and games to opening times, this is a must-read for every self-respecting pub-goer, from landlady to lager-lout.

978 0 7524 3994 5

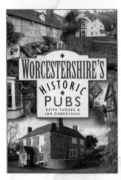

Worcestershire's Historic Pubs
KEITH TURNER AND JAN DOBRZYNSKI

This title provides information on sixty of Worcestershire's historic pubs including prime examples of riverside pubs – the famous Severn mug houses – wayside inns, canal and railway pubs, and home-brew pubs, as well as the mainstay of every community, the local. This book is a must for anyone who enjoys drinking and eating out in the county.

978 0 7509 4421 2

Visit our website and discover thousands of other History Press books.
www.thehistorypress.co.uk